PRAISE FOR
The Way of Quality

"It's fascinating! It's convincing! *The Way of Quality* shows us
the limitations of the conventional way we deal with change
and shows how the KAIZEN approach can lead to breakthroughs."

> MASAAKI IMAI
> KAIZEN Institute of Japan

"A striking message! It describes management and leadership
as a way of *being,* rather than a way of *doing.* No cookbook
prescriptions, but many questions that will stimulate rich
creativity in each of us to build capability in our organizations."

> JOHN CARVER
> Author of *Boards That Make a Difference*
> Creator of the Policy Governance Model for
> corporate, non-profit, and governmental boards

"I got excited when I discovered that this book was not about
processes and statistics but about our mental frameworks and
how we must change them for quality to work in American
business. Good job!"

> CHERYL C. JONES
> Founder/CEO
> Simply The Best

PRAISE FOR
The Way of Quality

"A first-rate look at 'thinking' improvements for any committed total quality effort. Tom's and Alan's dialogue conveys the essence—and importance—of Kaizen with clarity and simplicity."

> JOHN R. READ
> Executive Vice President
> Donaldson Company, Inc.

"Packed full of knowledge! It captures the very essence of quality. The dialogue format is extremely well done and very effective."

> MICHAEL E. SPIESS
> Management Consultant

"The common sense issues raised will take school leaders deep to the foundations of education. It helps us rethink our assumptions and provides new insights about transforming our systems to achieve total quality education for all students."

> DAVID M. HUTTON, ED.D.
> Superintendent of Education
> Lebanon Community School Corporation
> Lebanon, Indiana

The Way of Quality

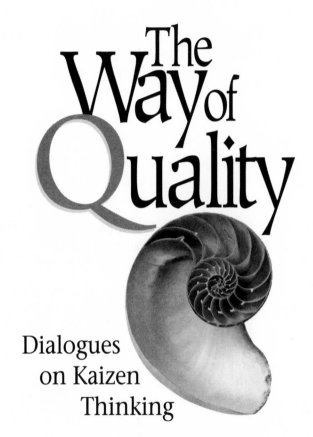

Dialogues
on Kaizen
Thinking

On the cover.
One of nature's most beautiful creatures, the chambered
nautilus adds ever-larger segments or "chambers" as it grows
throughout its life cycle. Kaizen-driven organizations are
like that; fed by nutrients from the environment, they
continually increase their capacity while maintaining
internal harmony and symmetry.

The Way of Quality

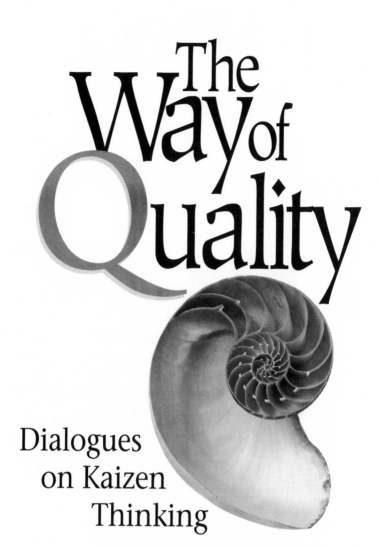

Dialogues
on Kaizen
Thinking

Tom Lane
and Alan Green

DIALOGOS PRESS

A BARD PRODUCTIONS BOOK

The Way of Quality
Dialogues on Kaizen Thinking
Copyright © 1994 by Tom Lane and Alan Green

Printed in the United States of America

Dialogos Press
5275 McCormick Mountain Drive
Austin, Texas 78734
512-266-2112 *(phone)*
512-266-2749 *(fax)*

ISBN 0-9636387-0-X

The authors may be contacted through:
Kaizen Institute of America
108 El Reno Cove
Austin, Texas 78734
512-261-4900 *(phone)*
512-261-5107 *(fax)*

A BARD PRODUCTIONS BOOK
AUSTIN, TEXAS

Copyediting: David J. Morris
Proofreading: Doris Dickey
Text Design and Jacket Design: Archetype, Inc.
Composition/Production: Archetype, Inc.

Prologue

Several years ago the Dalai Lama gave an address at a major midwestern university. He spoke extemporaneously for about 45 minutes, reviewing for his audience all the things he had seen in the United States and around the world that gave him happiness and hopefulness about the future. One was struck throughout his remarkable talk by the childlike clarity and playfulness of this great spiritual leader.

After the address was over, a reporter who had followed him on his tour asked the Dalai Lama how he could remain cheerful and undaunted in the face of so many problems, when he was still an exile after many years, and when he knew that the Chinese were doing their best to uproot and destroy the entire Tibetan civilization, including the religion that lay at its heart.

"Oh," the Dalai Lama replied, "you must understand that some problems are unsolvable. If they are unsolvable they are not problems. Other problems are solvable, so they are not problems either. Therefore there are no problems."

It is in that spirit that we have written this book.

Table of Contents

About the Authors

Tom Lane is a noted speaker and consultant for management and leadership of the organizational change process. His unique area of expertise is helping organizations make the transition from "short-term results only" to "world-class" operations.

Mr. Lane has been involved with management change processes since the early 1970s as an internal and external change agent in both the private and public sectors. He served as Director of Organization Effectiveness for Cummins Engine Company. Associated with the KAIZEN Institute since 1987, he has worked with various manufacturing and service companies including Goodyear, Ford, Donaldson, and Chrysler.

Alan Green, an authority on human resource development and organizational visioning, has pursued a lifetime career of learning and teaching in a variety of fields: business and industry, philanthropy, science and technology, cultural and intellectual history and religion.

Mr. Green's diverse background in business includes management positions with Macy's, Cummins Engine Company, and Schneider National, Inc. He has consulted with numerous clients including the Lily Endowment, Department of Interior, Goodyear, and Shaklee. He has been associated with the Kaizen Institute since 1988.

Setting the Ground Rules

This is a book about a major change that is taking place in the way U.S. leaders and managers do business, deal with each other and—most important—understand themselves. We, the authors, hope you will not find it necessary to agree or disagree with the contents—at least until after you have read it. To agree or disagree is to miss the point.

The New Game

We are attempting to describe two different realities that have nothing to do with rightness or wrongness, with correctness or incorrectness. Therefore, there is nothing to agree or disagree with. It is as if we were describing basketball and tennis, two different games each of which requires comprehension and understanding within its own context. After comprehending how the new game works one may agree to play or not, but it serves no more purpose to disagree with its rules than it does to disagree with the rules of tennis because they do not conform to those of basketball.

In the United States the automobile industry has been experiencing the effects of being in this new game for about ten years. Some call the game by the name of "unfair trade practices by the Japanese," some call it "innovative manufacturing," others say it is only the reapplication of old ideas, and some simply deny that any fundamental change has taken place—that the Japanese just work harder or are more disciplined than American workers, or that some other cultural difference accounts for their competitive edge.

If it is indeed a new game, what is the object and how is it played? The object, quite simply, is the ability consistently to provide ever-higher quality products and services at lower costs relative to the quality produced. This statement implies far-reaching, fundamental changes in the ways all of us view ourselves, our work and our relationships. In this society virtually all of us have a strongly embedded mental framework that insists that higher quality must cost more. In turn, this framework is tied to other assumptions or rules that make it extremely difficult to see how it can be otherwise.

In our capacity as consultants, we have observed U.S. firms struggling to attain high-quality, low-cost results. In the global market, those who have done so—many but not all of them Japanese—have been studied, written about, criticized and praised. However, we have seen few studies that try to probe levels deeper than the techniques and methods employed. It is as if someone wrote about tennis by describing only the strokes, and said nothing about rules or strategy.

Thinking Drives Action

Our view is that our thinking shapes what we humans do— that our manner of thinking, not only *what* we think but *how* we think, determines our actions. As we have sought to understand the thinking behind the methods employed by highly successful organizations engaged in global competition, we have found that the ways their managers and leaders frame their views of reality differ fundamentally from those of their "orthodox" counterparts.

All of us in business must learn a whole new way of seeing and interpreting our reality if we are going to be able to play the new game competently, much less become champions. Our business survival is literally at stake. Without a basic change of mental framework, we will never be able effectively to use the techniques and methods that have been developed as part of the new game, or learn to create new ones even better than those already in use.

To change the analogy, retaining the traditional ways of perceiving and thinking while attempting to make a business succeed in this new era would be like turning the command of a modern oceangoing vessel over to a captain who still believes the earth is flat. He might be expert at operating the ship, but would not venture far from port for fear of sailing off the edge, and certainly would never use the vessel to venture forth discovering new worlds beyond the horizon. And that is precisely what must be done.

New Mental Frameworks

This book, then, is about changing mental frameworks, what some others have called "mental models." What is meant by the term? To set the context, most of us believe that what we see "out there" in the world is what really exists. In fact, however, as brain researchers have demonstrated over and over again, what humans "see" is a complex of sense perceptions which pass through an elaborate and learned mental process. This process filters out masses of data and admits certain data which we have been taught to "make sense" of or recognize as relevant. But because these filtering processes are transparent to our senses—like very clear windows—we not only assume they are not there, we also assume that everyone else sees the same things and interprets them as we do.

Therein lies the difficulty. We tend not to look at the "windows" themselves to understand what they filter and change them if they no longer serve our purposes. Instead, we insist that what we see, and only what we see, is reality and cannot be changed. However, when we change our windows, what we see and how we see it can take on new and never-before-appreciated dimensions.

As one learns to see within this mental framework that constitutes the new game, three fundamental shifts make it possible to understand how to achieve high quality and low cost in every action taken. The first shift is from a purely externalized view of the world to one that combines internal with external.

In business/organizational terms this means not viewing business activity as strategic only, i.e., consisting entirely of externalities like market share, products and services, profitability, etc., but also seeing it from the perspective of capability: the internal ability of an organization to perform some complex of tasks effectively and efficiently. Only when that capability exists does one move to strategic planning.

The second shift is from a focus on content, or results—a focus that sees only *outcomes*—to one that appreciates the *process* leading to them, as well as the results. In business this shift involves paying attention to *how and why* something happens as it does.

Finally, there is a shift from acting in response to external crises or stimuli, to being internally driven by the freely chosen will to improve and create something better. In business terms this is the shift from what in this book is called "crisis-driven" thinking and operations—in which people react and respond to problems once they occur—to what we call "kaizen thinking," which includes but is not limited to preventing problems before they occur.

The Meaning of Kaizen

Besides "mental framework," a second definition is also in order. The Japanese word "kaizen" is conventionally interpreted as "continuous improvement" or "change for the better." These meanings are correct as far as they go; however, the word also implies making the changes or improvements through the active efforts of everyone in the organization. These efforts cannot be coerced; they must be internally motivated and freely offered. Moreover, kaizen implies a bias toward action. As one Japanese consultant has said, "Kaizen means DO IT!" (For this reason we have included exercises at the end of relevant sections which we strongly suggest that readers practice.)

Lest this point about action be misunderstood, it is important that we do not mean the kind of action typically taken by American managers caught up in crisis-driven thinking. There is no doubt that American business and industry is full of very active people, but their actions are almost always either reactive to some crisis or proactive to push some project through against the resistance of entrenched staff functions and bureaucracy. Action in a kaizen context is a different kind of action, based upon the mental framework sketched out in this book. It is action directed to performance of the work of the organization, and as such is grounded and practical. Typically, production workers in a factory or office quickly understand and appreciate the value of doing work within this new framework because for them it makes the work they do easier, safer, more challenging and more rewarding. In addition, they can see and appreciate the improved quality of what they deliver to their customer.

Understanding and Dialogue

True understanding comes only when thinking and action are combined so that one is able to see the effects of the thinking process played out in the external world of things and other people. Moreover, because perceptions drive actions, throughout the book focus shifts from the organizational to the interpersonal to the intrapersonal and back again. We continually establish that linkage and provide exercises and opportunities for reflection so that you can make connections of your own.

As will soon become apparent, this book is cast in the form of a dialogue between Tom, the teacher, and Alan, the learner. This has been our relationship for more than ten years, a relationship that has matured to the level of collegiality in which we give and receive insights and understandings from each other. Careful readers will observe that the learner does not necessarily agree or disagree with the teacher. Rather, he seeks to amplify, clarify, restate in his own terms, find practical application for the principles and concepts advanced, or in other ways develop fuller comprehension. Because it effectively shuts down the thinking process and replaces it with opinion, either agreement or disagreement is a symptom of the very reactive or crisis-driven thinking we believe must be transformed. Our purpose here is to model what we believe is highly effective learning in the kaizen-driven mode.

Regarding research, we did not use the currently accepted techniques and interview methods employed by academics and authors well known in business circles, since they capture only that world reflecting yesterday's mental frameworks and the leaders and organizations that have been successful within those frameworks. Instead, following theorists like Thomas Kuhn, we have endeavored to study the practices of companies and individuals who seemed to be, in Henry David Thoreau's terms, marching to a different drummer—hearing and seeing things differently, and doing excellent work excellently. Then we have gone behind their visible efforts to discern the ways in which they view the world in order to work in the ways they do. In order to show you that mental framework, we will use examples and descriptions common and familiar in everyday life to convey a sense of how this reframed world looks and acts. We have also related anecdotes from our own experiences in hopes that these may connect with yours.

We have developed and tested our insights and ideas over a period of ten years while consulting and teaching managers, chiefly in one major multinational corporation. We have learned much from our colleagues, students and clients, as well as from great thinkers in a wide variety of cultures and traditions—too many to acknowledge by name.

From our own experience, we believe that crisis-driven thinking and the systems based on it are obsolete, not because they are wrong or evil, but simply because they create problems that can no longer be solved from within that thought framework. The world must now be seen in new and different ways. When the industrialized world moved from the steam engine to other power sources, the steam engine did not become wrong. For most applications it simply became outmoded and obsolete. When Einstein invented relativity he did not make Newton's mechanics wrong, he simply pointed out its limitations. In organizational life old mental frameworks are passing into similar obsolescence. They are not wrong—in fact, in times of real emergency quick reactions are essential—they are simply inadequate to deal with the complex, interconnected systems that more adequately describe the way the world works. We must learn to recognize the new game, learn to play it according to its rules, and use and invent techniques and methods better suited to it.

CHAPTER 1

Beginning the Dialogue

A little over ten years ago, a group of about 25 managers attended a series of seminar/workshops. The purpose of these sessions was to learn better the thinking process required to lead organizational change.

Tom: Alan, I'd like to hear how you viewed those sessions. We never have talked about your early recollections and reactions.

Alan: Once a month I drove the 270 miles to attend what at first seemed like a series of mystery hours. I didn't have a clue as to what was going on. But because I respected you, Tom, I continued to attend. The sessions were supposed to be about thinking. Well, I thought, I can always stand a little improvement in that area, although I'm already a pretty good thinker. But the kind of approach we were being asked to take bore little resemblance to anything I was familiar with. The lecture sessions were hard enough, but the workshops were impossible. I remember being in several verbal duels with classmates who were just as sure they were right as I was that the truth lay with me. It never occurred to us that we all might have a piece of the truth. If it had, we might have broadened our perceptions to see a much larger picture beyond what any of us had seized on as the whole.

Tom: What caused all this confusion and frustration was the fact that all the managers were results, not process, thinkers. We have been trained all our lives to focus on *what,* rather than *how,* we think, so differences of opinion lead inevitably to impasse and conflict.

Alan: You were trying to get us to be "self-observing" so we could become "self-remembering." In plain English this meant that if we could be aware of how we thought, we might improve our thinking processes and thus our chances of achieving intended results. If we were only aware of the end product or results of our thinking—what we thought— improvement was impossible, for, as you continue to be fond of saying, "you cannot improve results."

The method you employed was that of slowing our thought processes down so we could be aware of them as they happened—hard work for a group who prided ourselves on being "quick studies." Throughout our school and work careers, all of us had been recognized, rewarded, and promoted for fast comprehension and right answers. But in this seminar the race went not to the hares but to the tortoises who slowly, steadily plodded along, checking our internal processes as we went. I can tell you that being a tortoise came very hard for me.

Tom: I know, but you stayed with it.

Alan: Then, after the first series ended, a smaller group of us continued to struggle with your latest "ahas!" We experimented with exercises designed to help us move along on the trail you were blazing. At the same time, as an internal corporate consultant, you worked with me on the change process at the plant where I was on the management staff.

By means of TOSS, our worldwide communications network, I would get short articles from you on various subjects related to process thinking, organizational change, leadership, and quality. You had been working with leading Japanese consultants and had visited companies in Japan, so you began to relate what you saw going on there to your own work on improvement. You included that in your writing as well.

I would circulate some of these articles just as they came to me. More frequently I would edit them a bit, adding some thoughts of my own. Occasionally I would TOSS in an article of my own, usually stimulated by something you had said.

More rarely, I would get together with you and one or two others and we would work an issue through, building on each other's thinking. Though they didn't happen often, these sessions were high points for me because in them we broke through the barriers our egos erect to the free exchange of ideas. There was no "ownership" or notion of "good idea" versus "dumb idea," but just the offering, receiving, reflecting, and synthesizing to produce new insights appreciated by everyone.

From 1985 to 1988 we continued to exchange ideas and articles from time to time. Meanwhile, I had begun to teach seminars and lead visioning sessions for top and middle management at the company where I worked. In these sessions I continued to practice, introduce, and expand on processes and ideas we had worked on or discussed. We also sought to translate these ideas into the creation of new company systems and structures that would support the new mental framework.

In 1988 you invited me to join you at the Kaizen Institute. We began to work together, mainly as co-presenters of the KAIZEN BASICS and LEADERSHIP seminar/workshops. You had done much to develop this curriculum, so a lot of it was familiar to me. Our times together permitted us to continue our conversations, usually over dinner at the end of the day. Topics ranged widely, from personal matters to movies we'd seen and books we'd read. But always we would be making connections, exploring how things that seemed trivial could resonate on very deep levels, and how the very deep could be revealed in the everyday occurrences of our lives. We were continually exploring and amazing ourselves with what Gregory Bateson calls "The Pattern that Connects"—the evidence of mental process and system running through the universe. This book represents a distillation of many years of reflection and conversation, alone, together, and with others, in a wide variety of settings. In this journey, you have led the way.

Tom: Thanks for the story. It's pretty much as I remember it too.

Alan: Thanks for the journey. It's changed my life.

As the picture of the chair suggests, we are inviting you, the reader, to join us in our ongoing conversation. We have included exercises at appropriate places to allow you to practice becoming aware of your own thinking processes. We have also set aside space at the end of every section for you to jot down comments and reflections as the third person in the discussion.

Two caveats. If you devour the book in one sitting, reading it as you would if you were only interested in getting the main points, you will almost certainly fail to develop the new men-

tal framework. To change how you think it is necessary to kaizen your process, and that requires practice, both of thinking and doing.

Second, those of you looking for "how to be successful" by using the current crisis-driven mental framework need read no further. You will not find out in these pages. But you who are searching may find help in discovering ways to reshape, re-think, reframe your efforts, and to learn better how to be fully awake and capable of acting purposefully in the present. At least that is our intent.

Although the book is divided into sections to facilitate ref-erencing, the themes are consistent, interrelated, and mutually reinforcing. Thus, if you wish, you may open at almost any point and begin reading.

After you have read and pondered and struggled and prac-ticed, at least a bit, we invite you to join our conversation by sending us your thoughts. In that way, our dialogue may become a multilogue that we hope can continue, expand, and improve—although in what form we don't know yet. Perhaps you'll have some ideas on that too!

Welcome.
Please make yourself comfortable
in the empty chair.

CHAPTER 2

Change in Crisis-Driven Systems

Alan: Trauma seems to be the main motive force behind significant change in Crisis-driven systems. We just don't seem to
make fundamental change unless we're faced with disaster.
Why is that? Why won't we or can't we see the need for
change when everything seems to be under control? Is it
possible to change without the spectre of calamity staring
us in the face?

Tom: As crisis-driven thinkers we have fixed ideas of how the
world should be. To us, what we *think* is right is what *is*
right. We believe in this content view, as opposed to a
process view, about the way things and people ought to be
and act. With a process view, we just watch ourselves and
others acting and see what happens as a result of those
actions. Then we make decisions about whether the results
are better or worse than another process might produce.

But in this crisis-driven mode we need—at least we think
we need—a fixed and prior image of good and bad, should
and should not, perhaps because we think that holding
these ideas about life somehow makes life that way. Or, if
we hold the idea of what's good strongly enough, we will
become good ourselves. Or, possibly, if I proclaim my idea
loudly enough, then the rest of the world will see that I am

right. In any event, the big payoff is that if I am right I won't have to fear being wrong anymore.

Alan: The televangelists come immediately to my mind. But I suppose that all of us fall into this trap as soon as we get preoccupied with being right.

Tom: Yes, this strong need to hold to fixed ideas about what's right and wrong in the world and in ourselves is a major block to change and a major source of blindness to what's really going on.

Alan: The irony is that we hold tightly to one set of fantasies because we're afraid of another set of fantasies we have—fantasies of a world that is not like the world we'd like to have. Meanwhile, there's the world and here we are, both very different from our fantasies. But we're too preoccupied with the fantasies to explore what's real.

Tom: With this crisis-driven mindset, changing means having to dismantle, partly or entirely, what we think is right. Since these fantasies you mention blur our view of ourselves and our actions, we don't really know if we do, in fact, follow our own rightness anyway. For crisis-driven thinkers it is more important to *know* rightness than to *be* or to *do* rightness. Thus the dismantling process is very disorienting because we are forced to act against what we *know* is right.

Alan: Whoa! Let me see if I've got what you're saying. As a crisis-driven thinker, I must submit everything I do or say or think to judgment about its rightness or wrongness. Now, though, I want to change the way I think because I can see that destructive or dysfunctional results have followed from my current thinking process and its consequent actions. But in the process of dismantling my old thinking framework I can no longer use my accustomed test of right and wrong, so now I feel morally adrift. I don't know what's right or what's wrong, yet my whole self-image is tied up in, and depends upon, knowing that I'm right. My uncertainty and confusion makes me feel wrong, because I should be certain. Yet I know this is the way I have to go in order to change.

Tom: That's it. You see, all change is to some degree "wrong" in our crisis-driven thinking, since we have such an investment in *our* way being the *right* way. To face being wrong is not only unpleasant, it threatens our very concept of self. For that reason, usually only a significant trauma will force us to change. Thus we tend to associate change with pain.

Alan: It's terribly painful to be wrong when we believe rightness is so much of who we are. I've spent a lifetime struggling to be right.

Tom: In fact, it's so painful that some change agents actually create serious crises which require change, then teach their clients how to deal with the pain. The problem with this approach is that the crisis-driven framework remains intact. In it, as we've seen, change is always painful and must be accompanied by severe stress. Another approach is to work on changing the total framework of thinking within which rightness and wrongness play such important roles.

Alan: But surely you can't be arguing for a totally amoral stance in life, where good and evil don't exist and we can do anything we want?

Tom: There are really two issues in your question. First, you've put your finger on the way we have confused the terms "correct" and "incorrect," "right" and "wrong," and "good" and "bad" or "evil." "Right" and "wrong" shade over both to the left and right so that we may call the answer to a math question "right" when we really mean "correct," or we may call someone "bad" when he or she has done something "wrong." This discussion has nothing to do with moral goodness or badness, except in the sense that crisis thinkers often see themselves in that light when they make mistakes.

In a kaizen framework of looking at the work performed in organizations, there is no question of rightness or wrongness, of good or bad. There is instead "the way it is" and "other ways it can be." "The way it is" asks you to notice things and have some valid data about how things currently work. There is no implied judgment of wrongness or badness. One may simply be curious about how things are working, much as a small child is curious about all manner of things in the world.

When you apply kaizen to production systems, you open various forms of data collection, formatting, and presentation for all to see. There are no hidden figures, no "fudging" to look good. Managers are willing to discuss how you and others manage and lead the operation, and how they themselves manage and lead, with a view to gaining self-understanding and improvement. All are accepted as being as capable as they can be at this moment.

Change in the kaizen framework comes through creating a sense of how things can be. "Can be" or "could be" is not the same as "should be." "Can be" is a statement of what our knowledge and imagination can currently see to be a better way of operating in the world.

Alan: I take it that "better" is not the same as "right"?

Tom: The key difference is that there is always a better. Right is final: there is only one right, while there are many betters, an infinite number in fact. Moving from how it is now to how it can be is a natural progression; at each step, how it is now is better than the way it was. We're not measuring better as an end state. We are only looking to see if the trend is moving us toward our desired end. So growth or improvement is simply change toward what can be. At some point along the way, the question will again be raised about the "can be" we are pursuing. Is it the same as when we started? With new knowledge and awareness we can, and usually will, imagine a new and better "can be." It is usually in the same direction, only farther out, more of a stretch for our imaginations and energies, and also more inspiring.

Alan: It strikes me that at the personal level, too, this combination of acceptance of who we are, while keeping an eye on who we can be, gives direction to our own development. As we grow and ask probing questions of ourselves, the "can be," let's say of wealth and power, may give way to higher purposes. Accepting where we are on the path lets us enjoy the moment, knowing there are more and more wonderful things to come.

Tom: Whatever energy we expend in struggling against who we currently are—judged by our notions of good and bad, right and wrong, which both come from and reinforce our feelings of inadequacy—can be rechanneled into positive energy for growth. Our ideas of what we can be become less like the external goals or resolutions we impose on ourselves, the medicine we hate yet tell ourselves is good for us, and take on the character of a self in the organic and internal process of continual unfolding.

Alan: Whew! This is pretty heavy stuff. Can we try it again from a slightly different angle?

Tom: Sure. We can talk about it tomorrow, but I don't want to lose the second issue you raised.

Alan: Which was?

Tom: The question about an absence of any kind of morality in the kaizen system. I see the kaizen system as authentically moral because it depends upon responsible choice, not upon received and untested rules of conduct. Our moralistic reactions to events are triggered by pre-programmed rules about right and wrong, good and bad, and they kick in before we really know what's happening or anything about its context. Our thinking shuts down and our responses become automatic, rather than the result of responsible choice.

Being clear-eyed about ourselves and our actions (casting the log out of our own eye) enables us to see the actions of others clearly as well. Then we are able to make much more solid distinctions between right and wrong, good and evil, and act as responsible moral agents.

CHAPTER 3

Crisis-Driven Growth

[The following evening]

Tom: We have all heard the saying, "No pain, no gain." It supposedly describes the difficulty we experience in growing or changing. From time to time some of us may have felt skeptical about that generally accepted wisdom. Certainly in crisis-driven thinking the statement is accurate. In a kaizen-driven approach, however, "no pain, no gain" does not apply: growth and change are natural and inspiring rather than painful. Those who say that pain is necessary for growth can't see how it can be different since almost everyone around them is also crisis-driven. To them the rule seems universal.

Alan: Why is there pain in one system and not in the other?

Tom: In crisis-driven thinking we judge everything we see and hear. (In fact, right now you may be judging this last statement.) Our mental judging process categorizes everything as good or bad, right or wrong. We believe that this categorizing allows us to manage and control ourselves and our environment—that unless we are constantly accepting the good and the right and rejecting or punishing the wrong or bad, the world will fall into chaos.

Alan: Do we really believe that we are that powerful?

Tom: So it seems.

Alan: Well, it certainly seems to apply to some folks' thinking about presidential candidates. If it's wrong to oppose a war we're in, or to smoke pot, then the person who does them is wrong and couldn't be a good president, no matter how much time has passed or how much change of thought and action has occurred.

Tom: That does sound familiar. The judging process requires that anything "bad" needs to be changed or rejected and anything "good" needs to be kept as it is. Ambiguities are unacceptable. They must be clarified so they can be properly classified. We need to fit everything in its right place, either this or that. For most of us, it is the only way we can experience a sense of certainty or stability in our lives.

Alan: There's a curious logic here. If, in this thinking framework, anything bad needs to be changed or rejected, then anything that needs to be changed must be bad, because if it were good it wouldn't need to be changed.

Tom: Exactly, and that is the cause of much of our pain. When we sense or are told that we need to change, we infer that we are bad or wrong, and that is painful. The pain of growth or change is this self-inflicted judgment. We believe we have to punish the bad parts of ourselves and drive them out—as if we could ever totally eliminate the "bad" and emerge as totally "good" people!

Alan: I know I torment myself with threats, chastisements, self-contempt, and other internal punishments to get myself to change, and then feel even worse when I backslide and have to begin again.

Tom: And all of this pain is unnecessary, because the whole mental framework is illusory, something we made up years and years ago when we were small.

In contrast, kaizen-driven change is stimulated by curiosity. We explore into ourselves to discover new options, new insights, and to find areas where we need to let go of old, ineffective habits of thinking and feeling. Bringing to light aspects of ourselves never before seen or admitted is an adventure rather than a plunge into hurtful self-deprecation. Change becomes automatic and natural as new light is shed on hidden areas and old dysfunctional patterns are released.

Once again, contrast this approach with the crisis-driven approach, in which we think we make ourselves grow, grimly asserting that we *will* be different—as if our wills were all-powerful and could be managed apart from the rest of us. This forcing notion somehow implies that stagnation is normal and growth and change are abnormal—that change requires extra effort—whereas just the opposite is true: *not* to change is what requires great exertion.

In this latter regard, much the same can be said of organizational systems. We use enormous energy to maintain systems as they were originally set up.

Alan: It's as though the people who invented the systems in the first place were gifted with great genius and made them perfect. So any change must be inferior to the original design, and anyone who suggests that a change might be in order is looked on as some kind of oddball or even saboteur. Proponents of change are almost always attacked with arguments based on the weaknesses of their proposals, but attention is almost never paid to the weaknesses of the existing systems.

Tom: Oddly, though, when a group of people experience change at work that they themselves have a part in bringing about, they feel pleased and excited knowing they have become more capable, more productive, and more powerful.

Alan: Yes, I believe the old observation that people do not like to be changed, but welcome change if they make it themselves and can see the benefit of it. What I particularly like about your last statement is that bit about capability and power. There's a lot of talk going around these days about managers "empowering" people, as though they deliver power, rather than just providing the opportunities and skills practice so people can get in touch with the power that's inside all of us.

Tom: Unfortunately, we have entire organizations of people who can only hear, see, and think in a crisis-driven mode. In such organizations, all change, no matter how it is managed, feels and sounds like blaming and judgment. Since crisis-driven persons want to avoid the pain of looking at themselves, they want to blame the stimulator or initiator of change, just as you pointed out.

Sometimes stimulators of change are judgmental, so they're seen as doubly threatening. But one of the amazing aspects of becoming kaizen-driven is that judgment no longer feels threatening. We simply recognize that some people operate in a judging way. When we stop judging ourselves and others, all judging stops, both *by* us and *of* us.

Now, Alan, please don't judge the truth of this statement until you have spent some time in a non-judging state.

Alan: Okay, you know me well enough to know that this is a timely caution. But I have been in many organizations that are full of highly judgmental people. If I'm the only one who drops his guard and becomes kaizen-oriented, won't I just become the target for everyone else's shots?

Tom: Being kaizen-driven in a crisis-driven system will be no problem, but thinking that it will may keep you in a crisis-driven mode along with everyone else. It's entirely up to you.

 Exercise in examining our own list of "rights." Take a few minutes to identify three or four favorite "rights" of your own—not rights in the sense of the Bill of Rights, but rights in the sense of "It is right always to tell the truth." Once you have done that, select the one that you feel the most strongly about, the one that it is never right to violate. Now ask yourself, why is this right? If you find yourself referring to some external authority like your parents or God or the Bible, put those responses aside and ask the question again until an answer comes from within you.

Why do you believe this principle or rule is right for you? Keep pursuing this question until you are satisfied you have discovered the "root cause" or answer.

(It may be that you cannot think of any reason other than that of some external authority. If so, you may want to re-examine the rule and ask yourself if you want to own it, that is, make it your own rather than simply accept it because someone or something said it was right. It may also be that you really do not know why you think it is right and are not sure you still believe it is—at least not until you experiment with ignoring or violating it to observe and assess the effects. When they perform this exercise, most people discover that what they strongly believe is right for them is so because they have experienced what happens to them when they follow—and when they violate—its precepts. In other words, it is right because life works better that way.)

CHAPTER 4

The Essence of
Crisis-Driven Thinking

Tom: All the variations of crisis-driven thinking and behavior are grounded in one simple, powerful mental process: *a rigid idea of what the world should be.* This is also the soil in which judging of self and others takes root. Most of us are taught from earliest childhood that there's a right way and a wrong way to do and be. For us as children, this "right way" has enormous power.

Alan: I'll say! I remember that when my parents wanted to impose their values on me, they would tell or show me through their tone of voice or facial expression that I was wrong or bad. For me, "right" always equated with "good," and "wrong" with "bad."

Tom: By the time I became an adolescent I was desperately trying to formulate my own set of "rights" and "wrongs" in order to regain some power over my being.

Alan: What today we call autonomy. It's essential for us as adolescents to do that. It gives us the strength to stand on our own, to have some integrity.

Tom: Yes, but at that time in our lives we usually don't see the price incurred if we don't move beyond our own teenage idea of "rightness."

Alan: At that age, maturity for many of us simply meant replacing our parents' "right ways" with our own. Frequently our right ways were not much more than reactions. My grandfather was a member of the Liberal party in Canada, my father was a Conservative, and a Republican when he became a U.S. citizen, and I am what some would call a liberal Democrat.

Tom: Then a lot of time is taken up arguing about who, and whose party, is more right. You become outraged when "the world" or someone else doesn't live up to the way it should be. You justify your positions, support them with facts, assault the intelligence and ethics of the opposition, waste your energies in a vain attempt to win the other over to your view. These positions we take are stimulating. They are also highly addictive because they march under the banners of commitment, patriotism, caring, sensitivity, justice and other noble concepts, concepts we are willing to fight and even sacrifice our lives for.

Alan: I can see that in my own life I have been strongly positional about what is and is not ethical, and have been very judgmental toward others and myself when we failed to live up to the ways we should act. But if this is the essence of crisis thinking, what alternative can we adopt to break the vicious circle we seem to be in?

Tom: One way to think of it is simply to change any idea of how the world *should* be to how it *could* be. The *should* framework assumes that one knows what is best for others, ourselves, and for the unknown future. The power of *should be* is the power of dominance and control. It is the power of dependence/independence, whereas *could be* is the power of freedom/responsibility.

Alan: What do you mean by that last sentence?

Tom: On the one side, the *dependent* side, *should* evokes in us our childhood desire to please the authority, whether parent, boss, priest, or coach, to gain unconditional love, the love we never felt. On the other side, the *independent, should* evokes the adolescent autonomy and tells those of us in power over others that we are right and they are wrong, and that as long as they are wrong we don't need them. We just move the voice of authority inside, and become dependent on that.

The *could be* framework talks to possibilities and potentialities that as yet are unrealized. The world *could be* many ways, and as we approach choices we look at the alternative *could bes* always with a higher question: does that path move us toward more of our collective potential for good?

Alan: It sounds to me like "moving toward potential" is something we *should* be doing.

Tom: It could be. Any statement can be a *should* or a *could*. The difference is the type of energy tapped by entertaining the *could* instead of the *should* thinking process. *Could* thinking opens us up to possibilities while *should* thinking closes us down, locks us into our narrow formulations.

Alan: I think I get it. *Could* gives me options as a creative subject, while *should* eliminates options, makes me an object along with everyone and everything else. *Could* reflects my will to pursue, helps me think about how something might work, while the way it *should be* makes me draw immediate conclusions without examination. With *could be* I get curious, with *should be* I get self-righteous or self-condemning.

Tom: That's the idea. In business we have both met many people who have definite opinions about how we should or must be. The fact is that any business could be any one of many different ways. Whether it survives, only time will tell. Those who are driven by strong *shoulds* think they can guarantee survival by doing things the right way. They love this illusion of power, and are fond of saying, "We must do this or we won't survive." Such certainty about the unknown and unknowable! The fact is, however, that even if we adapt and change in hopes of surviving, sometimes we don't survive. That's just the way it goes, no matter how we think it should be.

Alan: What I think you're saying is not that we should be *could be* thinkers, but that our possibilities of survival are enhanced if we consider all the various options, even though survival is never guaranteed.

Tom: Yes. For an organization to grow and live well it needs to be open to the many ways it can be. Crisis-driven thinking, based on rigid *shoulds,* diverts energy away from change and growth. And as you pointed out, using stronger *shoulds* to break out of crisis-driven thinking does no good. It's like throwing a bucket of water to a drowning person.

Exercise in imagining various ways that you could be. Make up as many scenarios as you can, visualizing in as much detail as possible how that way of being might play out. If you find yourself making any judgmental statements to yourself about what would be "wrong" or "bad" about being that way, note it and let it go so you can return to imagining that way of being.

At first you may have difficulty imagining any other way you could be. That's okay. Many of us are stuck on one picture, one idea of the world and of our "proper" or "right" place in it. Just be aware that to see the world this way is to be trapped by a lot of *shoulds.* Perhaps that is where you prefer to be. If not, you might begin with some experiments, like imagining what it could be like if you were exactly the opposite of how you are now, or imagining how you could be if you made a career out of pursuing your favorite pastime. Every time you see someone on the street engaged in some activity, imagine how you could be doing it.

Be aware that you are just playing. You are not obligated to report to anyone or justify yourself, so let yourself go and picture yourself doing what you want. Gradually you will begin to feel the horizons broaden out. The world of *could be* will begin to emerge.

CHAPTER 5

Crisis-Driven Listening

[In a seminar on Active Listening]

Tom: We waste a lot of energy in poor listening, energy that could be better used in learning or getting on with other activities. As I reflect on how I have developed my listening skills, the one thing that seems to account for most of my improvement is replacing crisis-driven thinking with kaizen thinking.

Crisis-driven listening is for the purpose of judging rather than comprehending. When we listen from a crisis-driven mindset, we are looking for flaws in logic, mistakes in data, wrongness of values or opinions different from our own. We listen only enough to "inspect" the issue at hand and then to declare our judgment or our areas of disagreement. Since our brains react more quickly than others talk, we believe that we can listen and form our presentation or rebuttal at the same time. Crisis-driven listening is a competition or contest of ideas. We each want to win this mini-event we call a discussion. When confronted with someone we believe we can't beat, such as an expert or an authority figure, we often turn our listening in upon ourselves and feel comparatively inadequate and stupid. We are apt to say that the expert makes us feel this way, when the fact is that we simply do not know how to compete to win. In the crisis-driven mode, all of life's interactions at work, home, and play can be seen as win/lose competitions and will seriously cripple our ability to listen and truly hear.

The kaizen approach to listening demands that we hear only what another person is saying. Our own added judgments and opinions have no place at the time of hearing, because without clear comprehension there is no place to begin a real dialogue. To learn how to hear the speaker we may have to use "active listening" techniques to help us get over our crisis-driven habits—although there is the added danger that we may pay so much attention to doing the techniques "right" that even more distractions enter in. Really to hear from the speaker's point of view, however, means that we must sacrifice our ego-based need to win or know better. It means taking the listening process out of a competitive framework.

Alan: What you're saying reminds me of your comments about presence. The kind of listening you're talking about requires that we truly attend to what the speaker is saying, and only that.

Tom: That's right; it's the essence of any true relationship. When we listen from a kaizen mindset, we're always focused on improving our ability to relate to others. We want to understand how they operate, how they see themselves, and what priniciples and beliefs constitute their framework of meaning—not for the purpose of manipulating them, but out of profound respect for their being. Most people want to establish their differences rather than take the time to comprehend another and discover common ground. When everyone is stressing his or her uniqueness, no one communicates with anyone, even though a lot of talking occurs—usually at higher and higher decibel levels.

Alan: Some may think that you are urging agreement with everyone. But I understand agreement also to be crisis-driven, as is disagreement. To listen for comprehension is to suspend agreeing or disagreeing until we have some data.

Tom: (Nodding) I find that most U.S. plants I've visited are crisis-driven. Very little listening goes on in them when production problems are discussed. Instead, people use factual data only sporadically, argue vigorously for their own opinions, don't try to understand the system from its point of view, and are primarily concerned with controlling outcomes or getting a majority to agree with them rather than understanding the processes that create outcomes. We seem to want to win more than we want to learn and improve.

In kaizen-driven plants, judgment is suspended as data are collected from all levels and analyzed. Judgment is replaced by choices of options for improvement. Who is right is not the issue as managers listen to what is going on between persons and on the systemic level.

Alan: When you say "data are collected from all levels," do you mean from all levels of the organization, or from all levels on which communication takes place, between people and within ourselves?

Tom: Both. Improvement requires listening to what others tell us and to our own internal messages. Debate is the game of a Crisis-driven system. It is fun but not helpful, except as an exercise for developing quick-wittedness in school. Learning to listen by following another's words and attempting to hear from her or his perspective is a way to slow down, or even stop, our judging. When we do this, everything we need to say comes of itself without our having to play it over beforehand in our heads. It is an energy-efficient way to listen, let the mind synthesize, and gain added perspective from a different viewpoint, all at the same time.

 Exercise in listening. As this piece points out, we tend to listen poorly because our crisis thinking causes us to cast judgments, either on ourselves or on others, as to rightness or wrongness. Three common reactions to what others say get in the way of clear comprehension. The first is thinking of a rebuttal to what we assume the other person will say or is saying. Second is distraction, usually because we consider something else more important to think about. And third is fear that we will not remember what the person is telling us—usually accompanied by taking notes so we won't appear to be stupid if we do not recall everything the person said.

Since learning to listen well requires considerable practice and feels awkward at first if you are a confirmed crisis thinker—and who isn't?—choose someone you feel very comfortable with and a setting with few distractions (a lunch room or cocktail lounge is not a good idea!) Begin by asking your partner to tell you about something relatively non-controversial, like a recent vacation or movie recently seen. As she or he speaks, picture what is being described; see it with your mind's eye. If a part of the picture is missing, ask questions until your partner is finished and your mental picture is complete. Then describe your picture to your partner. Take note of any inaccuracies or omissions that your partner corrects.

Keep practicing this method with different subjects. As your accuracy improves, begin asking your partner to talk about matters that you have strong opinions about. Do not agree or disagree. Instead, seek to discover everything you can about your partner's perspective: how she or he came to hold the opinion; what the underlying principles or values are that shape her or his approach; etc. Once again, the aim is not to have a debate, but to put yourself in your partner's shoes and see with your partner's eyes.

Depending on how much you want to improve your ability to listen, you should be able to notice considerable improvement in a half a dozen sessions. You may also note that you know your partner much better and feel much less anxiety about winning or losing, or feeling stupid when you forget something (you will probably forget a lot less, too).

CHAPTER 6

Crisis-Driven Learning

Tom: Once, during a workshop on developing the new thinking required for operating a kaizen system, a highly successful and competent executive pulled me aside. He asked me why he should work so hard on learning these new ideas when he was already more competent than the majority of his peers.

Alan: That sounds pretty arrogant.

Tom: Perhaps, but what he said was true. He was extremely competent, far ahead of his colleagues in most respects. I responded that the internal drive for excellence does not derive its energy from comparisons with others. I think that spoke to him, since he went on to accept more learning from the session. I tell this story because it brings to light another aspect of crisis-driven thinking—what it has done to our capability to learn continually. On the heels of that conversation, I wrote this short article. Please read it and give me your thoughts.

For the crisis-driven person, external necessity is the mother of creation and learning. Whether that necessity is competition or pleasing others or survival or getting a degree doesn't matter. The point is that most of us wait to learn or create until some discomfort is imposed. Once it's re-moved we lapse back into maintaining the status quo. Learn-ing for learning's sake is viewed as strange or a waste of time; if knowledge cannot be applied immediately to pressing prob-lems, then it has no value. That is probably why cramming for examinations is so common in even the best colleges and universities. We learn enough to get by, or to succeed rela-tive to others. "Relative" is the key word here, because it is the thinking produced in us by the bell-shaped curve. What most people want to do is to be on the right hand slope of the bell—not way out to the right—that is, excellence—or in the left tail—failure. We want to be better than average, the good strong B not the A or the "Gentleman's C." To learn more than the B requires would make us look aberrant.

When we regard the creations and inventions that have changed life dramatically over the centuries, we see that many have been made by people considered quite abnor-mal in their culture. These creative ones were operating from an internal vision, rather than from an externally imposed bell-shaped curve of normality.

Personalizing these observations, we find that learning about ourselves is often thwarted by a different aspect of cri-sis-driven thinking. The crisis-driven person usually associ-ates responsibility with blame—that is, if I do something that has negative consequences for myself and others, then I must be bad or wrong. Our culture seems to relish finding fault, rather than encouraging us to learn for improvement. Therefore, when we do things contrary to our espoused beliefs, we often deny responsibility because the self-blam-ing and judging by others feel too harsh and depressing. But such denial does not allow us to look clearly at how we are as a total human system. We develop significant blind areas that continue to drive our actions without our conscious knowledge, and so—like St. Paul—we do the things we hate over and over again.

Alan: I like what you've written. It occurs to me that in business we often do the same thing with data. We don't develop and use simple and clear data collection and analysis systems, since blame and punishment often follow "mistakes" and "failures" revealed by the data. When the data reveal lack of leadership and management capability, blame and punishment are even more likely consequences. We love to catch the boss in a mistake and then blame him for everything that's wrong—though we never say it to him. Bosses collude with this hypocrisy by not making it easy and constructive for themselves and others to review their behavior publicly. The whole organization gets stuck in a non-learning mode through this crisis-driven blaming process.

Tom: In a kaizen-driven organization or person, the need to learn proceeds from internal curiosity that has no taboos or sacred cows. All subjects are avenues for learning, comprehension, and understanding. We are not talking here about a process of forever contemplating ideas and never acting. True understanding never comes this way. We mean having genuine curiosity about the total system and how to improve it. We also mean holding an internal vision that inspires exploration into areas where we have no answers. Then we take action with purposeful efforts to move toward the results we envision, paying attention to our progress as we go. This process is creative learning, rooted in action and reflection, that is continuously expanding and growing.

Comments and Reflections

CHAPTER 7

Planning in Crisis-Driven Systems

[Part of a conversation at dinner]

Tom: I recently read an interview in which Larry Bird [the great Boston Celtic forward] was asked if he planned to become the best in basketball or dreamed of it as a child. Bird responded that he really never thought much about it. He said he just loves the game and has worked hard at becoming the best he could. This response is similar to those given by most of the people I've read about who achieve excellence. Crisis-driven interviewers look for the "concept-action connection," that is, they want to believe that plans or conceptual images of the future are the critical ingredients for action. They, like many of us, want to believe that if we just think about, talk about, write about, or wish for something, we will get it. Thinking about and wanting something play an important part, but excellence comes chiefly from developing a system and practicing the operation of it in ways that lead to excellence in action.

Alan: When you say, "develop a system," are you referring to something like a pianist practicing scales over and over again to develop dexterity and knowledge of proper fingering? Or to a football team running passing patterns until they can carry out their assignments in their sleep?

Tom: Yes on both counts. You can find examples of what I'm talking about in every field. The key in every case is a combination of a clear desire or powerful love of something and diligent practice of the systems required to perform something very well. Too often we stop short of the second ingredient—the 90% perspiration involved in genius, as the old saying goes.

I used to run career development programs that gave people the illusion they could plan their life/career—that somehow they could control the future events that would enable them to achieve their goals. I stopped running these programs when I saw that they encouraged people not to look at their current capabilities and capacities, or their current opportunities for movement and growth. Countless career programs reinforce the idea of planning to get what you want in life. Getting what you want is a fragmented view of yourself, out of context with the changing environment around you. The whole thought framework behind career planning and getting what you want is set up to resist and fight external changes that "knock you off your course." I found most people spending their energy trying to get back "on course" rather than adapting to their situation to further improve their capabilities.

Alan: I've had experience with these programs too. While I thought they were useful in helping people think more broadly and deeply about a lot of factors, such as what they really liked to do, what they did well, where they wanted to live, etc., the programs never did help people focus on what they could begin to do in the present to improve their skills and abilities around what they really did well and liked to do. So all the planning usually came down to grabbing the phone and looking for a job.

Tom: That was what I saw happening too. The folks you and I worked with were looking to the future and were concerned with earning a living by doing what they already knew how to do. I am not suggesting that there's anything wrong with looking to the future. Instead, I suggest that we need to look as best we can in our admittedly limited way toward the future, envisioning a way of being and doing that is capable of doing well in that environment. That is a *vision*. A vision is not a plan. A vision is not an end state. It is a holistic description (or internal visual movie) of action or behavior that for us is excellence in the future environment we want to adapt ourselves to and help to create.

Alan: So a desired profit level, or a certain personal income or two homes and four cars does not constitute a vision because there is no operational action described that can be practiced within a system.

Tom: That's right. When you have a clear vision in mind of something actionable, you can come back to here-and-now and get a sense of the gap between where you are and what will constitute your desired capabilities. Then change for improvement is simply ongoing, real time movement toward achieving your vision. There are no road maps, since life is not fixed like a highway. As you practice, you develop the ability to use opportunities and barriers to attain your vision. Sometimes detours are taken and pauses occur, but persistent effort toward vision in the context of current reality is the way.

Most crisis-driven businesses make elaborately detailed plans based on a few critical elements that the leadership believe will happen. Theirs is usually a reactive projection into the future. Then they try to make a "plan" that will take the company directly where they think it should go, disregarding the many blocks and opportunities that exist now or spring up in the near term. Almost inevitably, unforeseen events knock the plan off course, and instead of developing more capability to use that situation, they re-project the future and set new reactive plans.

Alan: In some companies where I've worked, we just chucked the plan out and hoped that the next one would forecast the future more accurately than the last. I have also found that most organizations' plans have nothing to do with envisioned actions, but with numbers: so much planned capital investment, so much inventory, so much in days' sales outstanding, so much in increased sales and profitability, etc.

Tom: A plan consisting of a set of numbers doesn't help people see how to make adjustments. Adjustments are made through actions, not through numbers. When you are driving an automobile too fast, you can't reduce the speed, indicated by numbers on the speedometer, without lessening the pressure on the accelerator pedal. Actions drive numbers. Visions of actions can provide guides for adjustments to actions, but without the actions no adjustments can be made.

Alan: This is a radical idea for most business managers, who are in the habit of describing end state results numerically, without a vision of operations that would produce those results. In fact, most managers don't know enough about how their current operations work to connect them up with the numbers they study.

Tom: That's one important reason why it's difficult to find executives who are extremely good, both at conceptualizing and at conceiving possible actions, then persisting in supporting necessary changes. This fact applies whether the actions have to do with the organization or with themselves as leaders. In a crisis-driven culture, the best crisis-thinking planners, if they're lucky and successful, will be moved into policy-making positions. Their very success in the culture means that they will become major obstacles to shifting to a systemic vision backed up by operating plans that tie together action and action adjustments. Strange as it may seem, the work of such planners has little or nothing to do with the success of the organization, because it is planning disconnected from the work that's actually going on—like the person who says she wants to be a doctor but does nothing to prepare herself for such a following.

In the interview I mentioned, Larry Bird described his persistent practice and adjustment through years of playing basketball. In this way, he created himself in the light of his vision—to be the best player he could be. Along that path he was voted Most Valuable Player in the National Basketball Association. Until the end of his playing career Bird's practice continued because he did not know the limits of his potential.

CHAPTER 8

Crisis-Driven Costs

Tom: High quality in a crisis-driven system equates with high cost. The most obvious contributors to that high cost are scrap produced, inspectors required to detect defects, breakdowns that slow or halt the production process, and the amount of redundant buffering inventory to ensure on-time delivery. These are the most visible costs of trying to achieve high quality in a crisis-driven system.

Another significant but less visible cost is that of maintaining control over others so the management can be "right" in their running of the business. Elaborate measuring, checking, supervising, and other controlling mechanisms add no value to the product but exist only to give managers the sense of control over the operation. Each of these control mechanisms is unintegrated with the others and usually sends conflicting messages about what the production system needs to achieve. So a hidden cost accrues around the confusion these controls create in the minds and actions of the people trying to make a product or deliver a service.

Alan: Ironically, the control these mechanisms are intended to provide is totally unfeasible even if it were desirable or necessary. Those of us who have worked in factories on the shop floor or who have been enlisted personnel in the armed forces know that there are countless ways we can get out of doing something we really don't want to do, or get around a regulation. If we work the way the bosses want us to work, it is because we want to work that way. Meanwhile, the poor supervisors have to spend 80% of their time filling out reports to convince their bosses that they have the situation in control. Talk about needless costs!

Tom: As another example, crisis-driven labor relations pit unions against management in a right-wrong struggle, while ignoring the common bond that exists through a joint interest in creating a production or service system that can sustain a livelihood for all stakeholders. The cost of a strike or slowdown never gets on the accountants' books, but the loss of sales, market share, employee and customer goodwill, and direct cost to the customer, depending on the product, is enormous. No one wins in such a situation.

Alan: As one businessman commented after a long and bitter strike at Caterpillar, "The union and the company fought and the winner was Komatsu." Product design that looks at the product purely from the technical view, without taking ease of production into account, can also lead to needless long-term costs.

Tom: Certainly. A kaizen approach to product development starts with a total system view, and places the designer in the shoes both of the production process and of the customer. The product must be designed to function well in the user's total environment, and at the same time to be assembled with as little difficulty as possible on the shop floor.

To grasp what is valuable to the user in the overall system can lead to designs very different from those that consider only the technical view or how to avoid negative customer reactions. The hidden costs of customer downtime due to problems with the product, aftermarket service problems, production problems, supplier problems, and application problems are usually not seen on the "bottom line." These are the longer-term impacts on real quality from the customer's point of view, whether the customer is external or internal.

Alan: Crisis-driven support systems create struggles between functional staffs about whose program or what answer best addresses current problems or challenges. Endless hours are spent in meetings and planning sessions in which we try to be exactly right about actions that will change before the ink is dry on the plan. I once worked in an organization whose planning process took ten months to accomplish. By the time it was concluded, history had made the plan totally obsolete, and then it was time to begin another planning process.

Tom: The kaizen approach of making things better embraces various approaches with a desire to try things out, see how they work, and make adjustments. The crisis-driven need to "know the right answer" before trying something out keeps us trapped in a game of planning and preparing—getting ready to get set to get started.

On a personal level, the judgmentalism at the heart of crisis-driven thinking exacts a heavy toll on the sense of confidence and competence of the entire workforce. Since being judged right is so important, downgrading, criticizing, nitpicking, disparaging, discounting, and questioning people's capabilities are ever-present. Life at work becomes a constant game of one-upmanship, and the necessary bridges between ideas and people are not built. Various approaches are not woven together, positive support and connections are not valued, competition rather than cooperation and teamwork becomes the rule. The cost in operating efficiency of these conflicts and failures to connect is unknown, but surely it is enormous. The most unfortunate effect, however, is the damage to the long-term mental health and well-being of the persons in the workforce.

Alan: Each person in the organization must be confident and competent in the operation of those systems in which he or she is involved. No one can do it alone. A personal desire to win at others' expense, to be the only hero and know all the answers, drives down interpersonal quality and morale which, in turn, negatively affects organizational effectiveness.

Tom: It's clear to me that businesses and other organizations that have functioned well have done so because they are based on an unspoken contract. Their people show up each day to work together to provide a place to learn and grow, to design and operate a system to serve a customer, and to make enough profit to survive and reinvest. When this contract is redefined as an individual struggle for personal financial and career success exclusive of others' needs, then the production system and the human relationships that make it work are jeopardized. We need to re-establish the original contract. It is the quality of mutual relationships that makes a quality production system work. And it is through the effective working of the production system that all of us can thrive as individuals.

Comments and Reflections

CHAPTER 9

Control in Crisis-Driven Systems

Tom: Control is essential in both kaizen and crisis-driven systems, but they are very different types of control. In a manufacturing environment, with kaizen we need to be looking for the causes or processes which, if properly controlled, will always have the effect of producing a perfectly made product. This search for orderly control of the myriad physical causes that lead to high quality and low cost is the intent of all improvement processes. We want to condition our factories to pursue excellence in all they do. It sounds straightforward and simple enough. The problem is that most of us attempt to control in a crisis-driven way, and that defeats our purpose.

In crisis-driven systems, some managers like the feeling of power that comes with dominating, checking, and controlling others. Others fear that if they do not control subordinates, chaos and confusion will result. While they may not enjoy the feelings associated with control, they enjoy even less the idea of not controlling. Whatever their motivations, both types have a major investment in control of others. What neither group recognizes, however, is that, except in a one-on-one situation, it is illusory to think that control is possible.

In his experiments on animals the famous Russian physiologist Ivan Pavlov noticed that dogs salivated whenever they were served their dinner. By repeatedly ringing a bell at the same time food was served, he was able to induce salivation even when no food was present. Most of us think that Pavlov controlled the dogs' behavior (salivation), whereas what he really did was to control their association process. He did not threaten or force anything on the dogs to control them; he noticed an activity (salivation), built a conditioning process to reinforce (food), and then built in an association process (bell with food). In short, Pavlov worked *with* his dogs to create a desired effect; he did not make them do anything.

Alan: I hadn't thought about it that way. In contrast, I've known bosses who wanted to stimulate changed behavior in their subordinates but didn't take time to work with their people, notice what they were doing, understand and explain what behavior was appropriate and why, then recognize and reward that behavior when they saw it. These bosses just wanted people to obey when they were given direction. At some time in the past, they learned that threats and punishment got compliant reactions, which they mistook for purposeful action. Since they associated power with reaction to their orders, these bosses were satisfied that they were in control when they got a lot of people reacting. Who was the conditioned one here anyhow?

Tom: Before we go on, let's be clear that behavioral conditioning does work. It is the most basic, by which I mean most primitive, driver of change in human performance. After all, we are conditioned from birth to respond to certain signals from our parents and others. But by the time we're a little older and more sophisticated, we know that there are much more powerful and effective ways of stimulating change. In spite of that, some people in positions of power continue to satisfy their needs for control over others by demanding and getting reactions. We might say that they have never outgrown their early conditioning. One leader I know says,

"When I can get my people to jump I know I am in charge!" This is the way people addicted to domination assess their power. On the other side, subordinates have been equally conditioned to react and respond quickly to voices of authority. The action and reaction usually have little or nothing to do with continuous product improvement or customer satisfaction. It has most to do with being conditioned to get out of the way, appease the boss, or cover one's flank. In cases like this, subordinates are internally motivated to act, but their motivation stems from a desire for security or even self-preservation.

Alan: On more than one occasion when I challenged this kind of power and control I nearly got fired.

Tom: Yes, it can get pretty risky. Once in a workshop I was confronted by a man who wished to control my actions. He wanted me to become angry—thought it would be good for me. (Controlling people are always controlling you for your own good.) He thought active expression of hostility was healthy for everyone, and since I was not expressing mine, he concluded I was not in a healthy state.

Alan: How long had he known you?

Tom: He didn't know me at all. What's more, he had no desire to know me. But he knew what was good for me, based on his own experience. So he tried to provoke hostile reactions in me by attacking my intelligence, integrity, honesty, manhood—anything that might push my button. When I didn't react to him, he got more and more furious. At one point I thought he was going to attack me physically. What I learned in this situation was that people with high needs to control others for their own ends can be dangerous when you don't play along with them. They have identified a great deal of their own self-worth with their ability to control others. To deny them this satisfaction can lead to aggressive and destructive behavior.

Alan: This need to control others, and the violence that follows its frustration, may be seen in the widespread practice of wife and child battering by men in our society. You're lucky you weren't a beaten Tom, Tom!

Tom: That's cute. In contrast, kaizen-driven control is control in collaboration with others toward a common purpose.

Alan: In Pavlov's case he was manipulating the dogs because their purpose was food and his purpose was scientific research.

Tom: That's right. When we talk about common purpose, we mean a purpose that is honestly shared by everyone. If we haven't established a common purpose and vision, there is no kaizen-driven approach. If we don't control with others, there is no kaizen-driven approach. Both are essential.

Alan: When you say, "control with," what are you and others controlling?

Tom: We're all controlling the processes that make improvement possible along the way we're going. Common purpose and vision create a shared desired direction for the entire group and enroll them in its pursuit. Control is shared with the energized group to do purposeful work to satisfy a customer. For leaders, "control with" requires gaining knowledge of where others are and what they are trying to do, so guidance and support can be offered. "Control over" only looks at some end point and disregards where a person is starting from. Crisis-driven threats, used to obtain higher-level, internally motivated behavior, simply do not work. Over the long term, as soon as the threat or checking is withdrawn, the motivation to comply also disappears. Kaizen-driven coaching and working with people for improvement are essential for long- and short-term excellence.

Comments and Reflections

CHAPTER 10

Kaizen Super-Ordinate Principles

Alan: "Continuous improvement" is one of those commonly used terms that sounds universally attractive—something everyone would want without question. So why, in spite of all our good intentions, do we continue to repeat poor performance year after year, facing the same problems and struggles with little or no improvement?

Tom: Perhaps it's because we are all caught in ways of thinking that work against improvement.

Alan: But I don't know of anyone who isn't in favor of improvement. So the ways of thinking you have in mind must undercut or sabotage those good intentions?

Tom: Yes, they do. The traditional thought patterns I'm referring to are what I call the "inspector mentality." Inspectors are conditioned to judge the results of various fragmented aspects of an operation. They exist in all areas of our daily lives as bosses, parents, judges, teachers, priests, and other authority figures. Because for the most part they are esteemed persons, we tend to respect and emulate them. Though we may not like to be inspected ourselves, we love to inspect and believe it's important to do.

It is what important people do and who doesn't want to be important!

Alan: I recognize what you're talking about, but isn't inspection essential to make sure that work is done right, that products are free from defects, that children behave, that laws are obeyed?

Tom: As your question reveals, the inspection thinking process must always look at an event or product after the fact, often out of context of the history and environment within which it happened, and judge its goodness or rightness. As inspectors we firmly believe that once we have made our judgments and others are informed of them, the necessary improvements will be made. Alas, such is almost never the case. Much more frequently, the judged product will simply be scrapped but the defective process that made that product will continue. The judged person will find ways of avoiding judgment the next time—but not often through improvement. Common tactics include blaming others and distorting or concealing data that might cast unfavorable light on performance.

Because it focuses its attention on things that have already happened, and on the perceived rightness or wrongness of those things, the inspection framework blocks us from paying attention to the present, which is the only time improvements in a process can be made. In such a thinking framework we cannot move toward total quality, which I define as "continuous improvement in every process, including thinking."

The first widespread saying about quality in our company was, "You cannot inspect quality into a product." While almost everyone repeated that saying, I observed that few really understood the thinking shift required to stop all inspection of the work of others as a way to achieve quality. Most continued to inspect the finished work of others as though what they were doing didn't contradict the very obvious truth conveyed in the saying.

Alan: Are you saying that inspection has a place, but that the people doing the work need to be their own inspectors simultaneously with doing it?

Tom: Yes, exactly.

Alan: Yet (I'm still wrestling with this issue) when people are new on a job—or when children are new in the world of their culture, or of arithmetic or some other discipline—inspection is needed to make sure they have proper guidance in how things are done. As I think about it, this inspection needs to be done while the learner is actually carrying out the new activity, or very shortly afterward, to reinforce the desired method and make it habitual.

Tom: That's correct. It's as though there's a temporary guiding hand substituting for the internal monitor that has to develop. But no business or industry or community can ever hope to become outstanding relying solely on this approach. The best one can hope for is conformity.

In an operation based on kaizen thinking, or system-wide continuous improvement, people work within a framework of three underlying principles. I call them "super-ordinate principles" because, while there are many other requisite principles, these three form the basic foundation upon which all the others are built. They combine to create a different viewpoint from which to see and give meaning to the operation of any organization. They literally change the reality experienced, whether at work or in the family.

Alan: Let's review those principles to make sure I'm on track.

Tom: The first is that *results are achieved through, and only through, processes.* To improve results the processes must change, but to change processes we must be aware of them. Process awareness requires that everyone pays attention to the *way* things are done. In business this principle applies universally, whether in meetings, on machines, on assembly lines, in offices, or in the tool room. Process awareness demands self-awareness and self-discipline. If we are not attending to what we are doing, *as we are doing it,* we leave quality and its improvement up to chance. Self-discipline is the ability to sustain our attention over time to the ways we think and act, as we are doing them, and to see to it that these are aligned with what we wish to accomplish.

Systemic thinking is the second super-ordinate principle. To think systemically is *to see the whole environment or all the critical factors involved in the issue at hand.* It is contextual, relational thinking. The issue might be as minute as the proper tightening of a bolt or cooking a dinner, or it might be as large as the operation of a factory or global business. A systems thinker sees the relation of things to things, of events to events, of people to other people. The language of systems is filled with connections, relationships, interdependencies, cross-functional effects, and feedback loops. I once heard a Japanese businessman say that he spent a great deal of time "knitting" his organization together. Compare this way of thinking with the traditional way, which fragments, analyzes, and breaks everything down into distinct, discrete categories and boxes. In the interests of simplifying, the traditional way attempts to deal with the world in small, manageable chunks, ignoring the surrounding context or environment. We all learned this approach in school. The bell rang; we shut our texts in this subject and moved on to that one. There was no connection made between them. Thus, early in our lives we were led to believe that we could manage and learn better if we isolated things.

Alan: To some extent this approach is necessary. In trying to think about how to tie all those academic subjects together, even today I have a difficult time doing it. Reality is very complex and ways must be found to make it comprehensible, especially when we are young and just beginning to learn things like arithmetic and languages.

Tom: That's true. Nonetheless, in the everyday work world the context and environment as a whole must be taken into account if we're to avoid unforeseen disruptions and dysfunctions. Managers who think systemically are constantly creating an environment that in all its aspects supports the process of doing total quality work.

Alan: And they do that by continually integrating the various functions of that process. I can see why that's necessary in the light of all the mischief created when one focuses only on a small piece of the action as if it's the whole enchilada. What's the third principle?

Tom: The third principle is that *everything and everyone is approached in a non-critical, non-judgmental way.* It is to see others and objects with the eyes of a very young child, that is, with wonder and curiosity and profound respect. Key to tapping the energy of people desiring to do kaizen is to stop all negative judging. Early in our lives, most of us learned to think in terms of who is right and who is wrong, and to dismiss or punish those we viewed as wrong. It's unfortunate that most of us still retain this mental framework, because its effect is to drive out the natural curiosity and desire of people to experiment to make things better. Curiosity about how things work, the natural curiosity of children, is replaced by cautious self-protection, fear of doing or saying anything experimental because it might lead to blame or punishment for making a mistake. The desire to make something better is replaced with the desire to protect our backside.

In highly judgmental operations, real problems are often submerged for years. When these problems finally surface, responsible managers are blamed for failure, people in organizational boxes are shuffled, and the so-called reorganization is presented as an improvement. In other situations endless time and energy are spent making up good excuses and "fudging" the numbers so the upcoming inspection (often called a review) can be passed with the least pain and punishment. All the while, the process and the system continue to operate with low quality and high cost.

[The next day, after he had reflected on Tom's remarks, Alan dropped by Tom's office.]

Alan: It seems to me there's a fourth basic principle that ties all the others together.

Tom: What do you have in mind?

Alan: The principle of harmony and partnership. I contrast that with our customary principles of competitiveness and rivalry.

Tom: I'm glad you brought that up! I have taken that element so for granted that I omitted mentioning it. While I've always thought of it as harmony and balance, I like the notion of partnership too. How are you thinking about how these relate to the others?

Alan: Well, I haven't really thought it through, but let me try it out. Take process and results. Not only do processes lead to results, but those results have integrity with the very processes that create them. In other words, by following a certain process, you can't avoid getting the inevitable result. Now, integrity is not harmony; it's structural, whereas harmony is aesthetic. But if something is harmonious, it does have integrity. An example would be a work of music played by a symphony orchestra. If all the musicians are well trained, have musical "ears," and are attuned to one another, if the score is written by a gifted composer, if the conductor knows and loves the piece and has rehearsed the orchestra well, and if all the participants are thinking of themselves as partners in harmony, then the actual performance—the result—will reflect the processes that went into making it. On the other hand, if the basic underlying principle is competitiveness and rivalry, you could have exactly the same ingredients and produce a horrible cacophony, every musician vying with the others, defying the conductor, interpreting the score according to her or his own whims, etc. In such a case, the result once again would be integral with the process, but harmony would definitely not be the result.

Tom: My ears hurt just to think of it! And when we look at systems thinking, it occurs to me that many contemporary scientists are arguing the case for a "harmonious universe," in which all things, even the most minute particles, are bound together in a kind of vibrational dance. Whether we like it or not, the major problems of our world—population, pollution, fossil fuel consumption, food production and soils, the growth of cities, depletion of the ozone layer are all related to each other in a state of imbalance and disharmony—indeed, of disintegration, with potentially disastrous consequences.

Alan: There does seem to be a strong positive relationship between integrity, harmony, and balance.

Tom: I like to think in terms of dancing, and that suggests partnership.

Alan: When you mention dancing, I think of the Olympic ice-skating pairs. Imagine what would happen if their basic thinking principle were rivalry and competition with their partner! There would be no partnership. Those pairs are beautiful examples of integrated systems based on partnering, balance, and harmony—the whole being greater than the sum of its parts.

Tom: Absolutely. Okay, now let's look at non-judgmentalism and non-blaming. Do we have the underlying principle of integrity, harmony, balance, and partnership? What comes to my mind there is that if I feel competitive toward someone else, I am always comparing myself to that person. If I note differences, I tend to ask myself, "am I better or worse than Joe or Sam?" If better, I tend to judge Joe or Sam as not as good. If worse, I judge myself. But if I think of them as partners, working out of an integrated center in harmony with themselves and with me and vice versa, difference is just difference, not better, not worse. In fact, we appreciate each other's strengths as complementary and balancing. And when we think of partnership in this way, the ethical dimension of integrity also comes into play.

Alan: How do you mean?

Tom: Well, one of the biggest fears people have about partnerships is that one "partner" is going to abscond with the funds or in some other way leave the other partner holding the bag. So when we talk about people working out of an integrated center, in kaizen thinking we assume the center or core is ethical—that is, it will act with integrity towards self and others.

Alan: Let's see if we can put all this together. Harmony, balance, and partnership are essential underpinnings for the three super-ordinate principles, and they are all tied together by integrity, which we understand in both the structural and ethical sense. Could we say that harmony is the aesthetic dimension, balance the structural dimension, and partnership the ethical dimension of integrity?

Tom: Yes, I like that. Then we can think of harmony, balance, and partnership as the ground in which the foundations of the super-ordinate principles are laid.

Alan: Here's an afterthought. The term "partner" has become a buzz word in the business world in the last few years to describe all the members of an organization. Do you suppose there's any substance behind the word?

Tom: Time will tell. It seems to me that partnering is an outgrowth of, and a means of, working in harmony and balance.

Those organizations where all the members are called partners should, if there's real substance there, be marked by increasingly harmonious relationships. Not that all conflict will disappear, but it will be managed with a view to true reconciliation, not just putting salve on the wounds. For example, union-management relations will move from an adversarial stance, where one side "wins" and the other "loses," to one of advocacy and subsequent agreement where both sides win.

Alan: That would be a change for the better! And what about the trend toward hiring "temps" instead of permanent employees to avoid paying benefits and layoffs during business downturns? How can partnerships form out of such a practice?

Tom: If the temporary status is imposed on the employee, and he or she has nothing to say in the matter—in fact is often employed by a second company—then I believe partnership is impossible. But, as I said before, time will tell. Meanwhile, let's watch the process and see what results come of it.

Comments and Reflections: What key principles is your organization founded on? What are these principles grounded in? What kind of culture has grown up as a result?

CHAPTER 11

Crisis-Driven to Kaizen

[E-Mail message from Tom to Alan]
Hi, Alan, here's a piece I've written on the transition from Crisis-Driven to Kaizen. Let me know what you think of it.—Tom.

One of the major shifts underway in U.S. business is from an operating system that fixes a product or process when a failure occurs to one that creates the product correctly the first time.

Although it is often called the "prevention" or "continuous improvement" system, I prefer to think of it as the "kaizen system" because the Japanese word, *kaizen,* embodies both the principle of improving and that of involving everyone in the organization. This shift is being applied primarily in the shop-floor production of material, but it appropriately pertains to every aspect of the work carried on in human organizations.

The older crisis-driven system waits to check the outcomes of a process to see if the quality is good. Inspectors do this checking inside a company and the customer is the ultimate inspector. When defects or failures are found, energy in the form of reports, complaints, reject-and-return processes, tagging, and so forth is expended to seek out the guilty and fix the problem. Quite often the fix is not appropriate or lasting. Significant cost is always incurred because of the amount of processing that has already gone into the product by the time failure is discovered, and the number of people who must be involved to detect, report, and correct the defect.

The kaizen system is based on the idea that if you put all the correct factors in place and control the creating process, you will always create quality. Inspectors are unnecessary when you train people to understand how the production process works and how to maintain it.

Different ways of thinking underlie these two approaches. Crisis-driven thinking controls how most of us behave. It leads to managerial systems based on the assumption that people and processes will fail if left to themselves without

MENTAL FRAME	CRISIS-DRIVEN	KAIZEN-DRIVEN
Psychological Need	To be right and best.	To be improving continually.
Method of Perceiving	Looking at results with desire to control outcomes.	Looking at process to increase comprehension and performance.
Object of Measures	Fix blame, determine what/who is wrong.	Get data on current performance to help improve and adjust.
Source of Mental Energy	Threats/fear, fire-fighting excitement.	Problem elimination, challenge to improve.
Psychological Reward	Short-term fixes, immediate feedback.	Long-term system upgrade, indirect feedback.
Attitude toward Change	Avoid major system change because it implies wrongness.	Expectation of constant small and large changes.
Guiding Principle re: Change	If it ain't broke, don't fix it.	It can always be done better.
Learning Approach	Quick analytical skill and remedial action.	Curious about large system; act to create quality, prevent recurrence.

control from above. The table on the previous page contrasts crisis-driven and kaizen-driven thinking.

In the crisis-driven system, large amounts of human and machine energy are consumed to keep the system working but not improving. In contrast, the kaizen-driven system continually demands less and less energy. Excess energy is now used to make even more improvements.

Desirable though the shift from one system to the other may be, the transition must be made carefully. The crisis-driven system requires ongoing attention, even while it is being phased out, because it lies at the heart of all our current systemic structures and still maintains order.

[Follow-up telephone call from Alan to Tom]

Alan: Hi, Tom, this is Alan. I'm calling to respond to your piece on the transition from crisis-driven to kaizen. Do you have some time right now?

Tom: Sure. Go ahead.

Alan: I can see that crisis-driven thinking underlies how we measure things, develop people and information systems, deal with customers—virtually everything we do in our institutional life. So-called "human development" in the United States has been shaped by crisis-driven thinking, beginning with the formal educational process, if not before. The message in school is to get the best grades, not to enjoy learning and improving what we do. We test to find the successes and failures, not to learn how to improve. Not to do well in college is met with threats of course repetition or the axe.

Tom: Yep, and at work the same process continues. Outstanding individuals are rewarded with immediate raises and promotions, while being part of a larger improving or deteriorating system is disregarded. Learning is for those who have not "made it." Therefore, to confess that we don't know or must learn is to admit failure or inadequacy. Change is what others need to do who aren't as right as we are. We can talk of developing people so long as we are not among them.

For most of us, success demonstrates that we do not need further learning and development. Moreover, we don't have time to develop anyone else; we need action now. We know what is wrong because we can see others' failures, and we shouldn't have to understand the system or them for it to be fixed—that's their responsibility. Ability is a given: people either have it or they don't. We're always searching for the perfect person who "has it all."

Alan: I think these last statements are important and should be included in the body of the article. You might also want to use a letter from my file that I believe illustrates how crisis thinking leads to flawed perception, waste work, and stagnation of efforts to improve.

Tom: Good. How long is it?...Can you read it to me over the phone?

Alan: Yeah, here it is.

Dear Boss:

I came back to the department the other day just to say hello to some of my old office mates. In the course of our conversation I learned that you have been criticizing my replacement because he has let the backlog of work build up again like it was when I came into the job. They told me you have been saying you'd like to have me back on the job because I was such an outstanding performer.

Since I've been gone, I have thought about what I did in that job to get it under control. It was not that I was some kind of superman or anything like that.

You'll remember that when I came on board there was a six-week backlog piled up on my desk. Your instructions to me were to get rid of that backlog. Well, after I learned the procedure I realized that a lot of the data I was supposed to record wasn't required by anyone, so I went to the guys who filled out the reports and we agreed that they would just ignore those unnecessary items. That saved both of us a lot of work, speeded up my process, and I was able to eliminate the backlog in a matter of weeks.

You were delighted with my performance, gave me a promotion and a raise, and I got the nod when the department I'm now in was looking for a managerial candidate.

At the time it didn't occur to me to get the forms changed to reflect the new procedure, so I suspect that when the new man came in, he called attention to the partially filled-out reports and got people to revert to the old practice.

The point is that at first neither you nor I paid any attention to how I was going to get the results. You just said, "reduce the backlog." Faced with that assignment I had to figure out how to do it, but both of us were still so results-oriented that I didn't take the process seriously enough to document it. And when you treated me as some kind of hero, gave me a raise and a promotion, who was I to point out that I had only simplified the procedure?

Tom: That's a great letter. Please send it along. You know, having been in the development field for almost twenty years, I've seen many such cases. I have come to see that kaizen thinking is the only source of true development. Crisis-driven thinking is lazy thinking, because it waits until problems or failures arise before any efforts are made to correct them, while the kaizen approach demands work when things are going well. It also requires a much greater and deeper understanding of how things and people work, since we must go beyond repeating yesterday's fixes. It demands a will to improve and learn that pushes us out of maintaining the status quo and into creating new and better systems and cultures.

Alan: Speaking of waiting for problems or failures before acting, I continually see people unprepared for what happens to them in life. War, death, loss of jobs, old age, divorce—all catch them by surprise. Some of these events can't be planned for, but you seem to be saying that kaizen thinking helps us play an active role in creating the future we want, rather than our just being passive recipients, reactors to whatever comes.

Tom: Yes, I am saying that. Most of us simply react to life's crises as they arise, with no preparation or understanding that change is the natural order of things. We entertain the illusion that the good times will last forever, that once something is fixed it should stay fixed, that life is unjust when it doesn't turn out "right," that is, to suit us. In the face of change we are, first, passive, then reactive, then resentful (or happy), depending on what happens to us, not because of what we choose to do.

Moving to kaizen thinking is difficult but possible. We are responsible for creating, not waiting. Creating of ourselves a learning system based on kaizen thinking is the only pathway to whatever real security there is. The world will continue to offer us new challenges and opportunities as we actively seek them out, even in the midst of surprises.

Alan: I'll mull that over and we can talk more about it. Good to talk to you, Tom. Take care.

Tom: 'Bye, Alan.

Comments and Reflections on the idea that we can play an active role in creating the future. What about chance and accident, or forces beyond our control? How do we square this idea with events that take us by surprise? _____

_____
_____
_____
_____
_____
_____
_____

CHAPTER 12

Drivers in Crisis-Driven and Kaizen Thinking

[E-Mail message from Tom]
Alan, here is a list of what I call key drivers of action behind crisis and kaizen thinking. Any additions?—Tom.

Crisis Thinking	*Kaizen Thinking*
After the fact	Before the fact
Event-focused	Process-focused
Judgmental/critical	Curious/investigative
Right/wrong-based	Data-based
Non-systemic/narrow	Systemic/broad
Short-term fix	Long-term change
Expedite out-of-control operation	Upgrade in-control operation
Immediate/direct reward	Long term/indirect reward
Immediate problem fix	System/operation improvement
Minimum diagnosis	Continuous thorough diagnosis
Work/problems come to you	You go to the system
Internal—hero oriented	Customer oriented
Narrowing of thinking scope	Raising/widening of scope
Time to redo	Time to do it correctly
Progress is tangible only	Progress often intangible
Working harder gets it done	Working smarter gets it done

Crisis Thinking	Kaizen Thinking
Variance to fixed standard	Standard continually upgraded
Fragmented jobs	Work as unified flow
Disconnected individual effort	Connected joint effort
Things always break	Things are prevented from breaking down
Don't fix it if it isn't broken	It can always be improved
Give me simple answers now	Let's see how this works
Don't ask questions—do it	Questions help us understand
Don't confuse me with data	What are the data?
Job security comes from their depending on my ability to fix	Job security comes from increasing our capability
Learning takes too long	Learning is continuous
Learning means you are inadequate	Learning is necessary to deal with change
Getting by is good enough	Fixing it permanently is the only solution
Quality is passing inspection	Quality is no variances
Quality is not as important as Quantity/low cost	Quality is all there is
Quality is hardware	Quality is in everything we do and think
Don't challenge the system	Everything can be improved
Success is individual	Success is of the whole
Work manages me	I manage my work
Customer reactions drive improvement	Customer input blends with technology and capability input to create improvement
I get paid to react quickly	I get paid to think, then do
Who is to blame is important	What went wrong is important
Targets are to be hit	Trends of improvement are tracked
Don't worry about the big issues	Work on seeing how large issues affect the small ones and vice-versa
Mistakes mean failure	Mistakes show where we need to improve

Sources and Kinds of Energy Manifested

External stimulation from crises (especially bosses)	Internal stimulation from exploring discovering, improving, under-standing
Physical energy dominates	Mental energy dominates
Bored with discipline, routine, energy goes into complaining	Dislike disorder, maintain orderliness; cleanliness, standards, safety; self-managing

Comments and Reflections: *What additions can you think of?* _____

_____

_____

_____

_____

_____

_____

_____

_____

CHAPTER 13

Coming to Our
Senses on Quality

Tom: Managers in the United States are finally beginning to appreciate what it takes to produce quality in products. For years we have resisted adopting well-known and—in Japan especially—well-used systems and techniques. That resistance is starting to crumble as managers realize that the game has changed. To survive into the future, high quality with low costs is the only option.

Alan: What can we learn about this resistance to the pursuit of quality as the major driver for excellence? Why has it been so hard for us to accept? Surely it's not an accident, and I know it's not stupidity or laziness.

Tom: At the outset it's important to recognize that for years the market did not demand high quality and low cost. Financial success was possible without this combination because the United States dominated the industrial world in the decades after World War II and we could sell whatever we could make. Then the competition changed and so did the game. A recital of these external reasons is usually as far as most commentators go in explaining why the United States has lagged competitively. As I said earlier, I believe there are fundamental issues regarding how we think and perceive that have fostered a kind of thinking about quality that does not help us play this new game.

The essence of quality is creation. Quality is "built in," as the ads now say. To be built in means simply that the moment of creation of a product is the only time any real quality can be achieved. (This is also true of all other aspects of work, but for the moment let us stay with hardware.) Quality can be created only at the moment of taking action. This is so obvious it sometimes escapes our notice. The moment a cutting tool touches a piece of metal, it either cuts it exactly at the correct place and creates a quality cut, or it deviates and produces a defect. The moment in which a sales person conducts a transaction with a customer is crucial for leaving that customer satisfied or dissatisfied with the service received. Once this moment is past, an inspector can only comment, judge, or grade the result. The inspector adds absolutely NO VALUE to the creation process.

An inspector may protect the customer from receiving defective parts and may provide data for improvement to an operator or salesperson. That function can be useful. But in no way does after-the-fact inspection create quality. This point is very important to grasp fully. Quality is created, or not, in the moment work is performed *and at no other time.* Grasping this fact is essential for beginning to understand why so many U.S. companies have not been able to move as quickly as necessary toward improvement.

Alan: You are saying that it is of paramount importance to understand quality as a moment-to-moment creation?

Tom: Yes, simply because if we are not in touch with ourselves and aware through our senses of what is going on around us in the immediate present, we cannot possibly create quality in anything, no matter what we are doing.

Alan: Okay, I see that. Yet for years we have told others, and believed ourselves, that here and now are not important. The "bottom line" is important, whether quarterly or annually; the number at the end of the day's production is important; conceptual plans and strategies for next year are important. But seldom have we heard anyone say that RIGHT NOW is important. (Offhand I can think of only one exception, the professional driver trainer who taught our fleet drivers the safe operation of over-the-road tractors and trailers. He was intensely present-focused!) Everything could be put off or caught later and corrected. We could rework or catch defects. We could find time later to talk to our suppliers about their careless work. Yet the undeniable fact is that it is only in the here and now that quality can be created.

Tom: On machines we now use sensing devices and statistical process control to stay aware of real-time action so we can begin to operate in a way that continually improves our ability to create quality. The reason we took so long to use these techniques after they were developed is that few in our culture valued the present. If the present is not valued enough to be aware of it, then what's the point of process control?

Nowhere is failure to be fully present more apparent than in management. Most successful managers I have met are out of touch with their senses. In discussions they cannot listen to what is actually being said. Instead, most of them listen with an "inspecting mind" that constantly judges or critiques the words and compares them to their own internal version of what is "right" or "wrong." They cannot see what is actually happening. They can only see whatever fits their current framework, and think that is what others ought to see as well. They can no longer feel and respond to those current sensory and intuitive messages telling them that something is terribly wrong with the way things are going.

Alan: That certainly describes my own conduct for most of my life in management. Because I was not aware of the here and now, I missed the creation opportunity time and again. The amount of rework and scrap my colleagues and I created in our offices would never be tolerated on the factory floor. (An example of rework would be redoing plans and reports; of scrap, the number of meetings that led nowhere and accomplished nothing.)

Tom: It's important to point out that you and your colleagues were not bad or stupid when you performed your wasteful work. You were merely playing out the pre-programmed tapes of how managers are supposed to act. You were caught up in your past conditioning and were not aware enough to break it.

To create quality in management, managers literally have to *come to their senses.* They must start listening to themselves and others openly, without all the inspecting, critiquing, and pre-judging. They must simply see what is going on without having to make it conform to pre-formed images. Once they are sensing data, they can make correcting adjustments just as machines do, only better. Without conscious awareness in the moment, there is no possibility of creating a quality organization. And that, after all, is the appropriate work of leaders and managers. Managers do not make products; they make organizations that make products or deliver services. (I am amazed at how often I have met managers who, if they have ever known it, have forgotten this fact.)

For an organization to have high quality and low cost, someone must start the creation process right now by taking the focus off next week, next month, or next quarter, and become present with the organization as it is. Effective managers and leaders do not dwell on wishes or "if onlys." They are present with and to their organizations, sensing moment-to-moment opportunities for creating quality in the relationships, systems, and processes that form the infrastructure of organizational life. They have abandoned the old inspection and judging processes as they have come to their senses and begun to create quality.

Exercise in Being Present: Watch for a situation where two or more people are in a strained or heated discussion. Observe and listen without taking sides. Notice the body language, tone of voice, facial expressions of the participants. Simply take note of these "sense data" without intervening in any way. Practice doing this several times before you attempt to observe yourself in a similar situation.

CHAPTER 14

Process
and Content

Tom: Besides the fact that we have been taught that the future and past rather than the present are important, there is another significant barrier to our being present to the reality going on in and around us. It is what I call a "content/thing" focus.

Alan: "Content/thing" is an awkward term to me. What do you mean by it?

Tom: Content/things, like results, are points abstracted from within ongoing processes. Process contains content/things, but content/things do not contain process.

Alan: What are the main differences between these two, process and content/thing? What are the implications of a change of focus from one to the other? How does one go about making that mental shift?

Tom: Interesting questions. Most of us seem to focus on content/things as the main building blocks of our experience of reality. We look outward at the world and notice various objects, events, people as they come into our field of awareness and treat them as totally separate phenomena, unrelated to one another. We don't make connections between all those objects and events as elements of a unified whole.

Alan: Like the way a little child, just learning to talk, points to something and says, "tree," then to something else and says, "dog?"

Tom: Yes, very much like that. These things are separately classified and catalogued as having certain meanings derived from experience or from something we have been taught, that is, good/bad, right/wrong, friendly/unfriendly, important/indifferent, and so forth. The content/thing-focused mind is driven by comparisons between the current and past experiences of similar things or a mental image of the preferred or ideal thing. But it omits the historical context (where and under what circumstances the similar thing occurred), the current context (what is affecting this thing now), and the future context (what is helping or hindering the becoming of this thing).

Content/thing-focused minds tend to see reality as a kaleidoscope of changing problems and events disconnected from each other and from their environments. Obviously none of us can be purely content/thing-oriented and manage our lives very well. Imagine, for instance, trying to drive to work paying attention to traffic conditions, pedestrians in crosswalks, oncoming vehicles, or rules of the road *one at a time!* And yet some individuals live their lives very much like this, almost totally reactive to each external stimulus as it occurs. Whatever demands their attention most urgently gets it, and life consists almost exclusively of coping.

A content/thing focus sees life as a static array of goals, objectives, conditions, and end states. Reality is defined quantitatively: how much; how little; how many; due dates; bottom line. It is as if one were trying to understand a given historical period by looking through a collection of random photographs.

In contrast, the process-focused mind looks at things as they are connected to other things over time and space.

Nothing is taken as it is without placing it in its context of time, background, and direction. Also, process implies the movement of things in a changing state. Nothing is fixed, although the process-focused mind can use fixed points to mark progress, much as mile markers show progress in driving down a highway. But the marker is never confused with the process of getting to a desired destination.

A process orientation toward the world is quiet and watchful. It is not a thought or concept *about* what is going on; it is simply attending to what is happening and being absorbed in it. Process awareness notices changes, interactions, movement, and context. From that noticing, many content/things or results may later be selected and conclusions drawn.

Alan: I see. With process focus, we look at how things are moving with respect to where they were and the trend or direction they appear to be going. We base our judgments on direction and efficiency of movement, rather than on ideal states or static positions. In that way we experience a broader context within which to understand how things come about and change.

Tom: Yes, that's the benefit we derive from looking at process rather than at things. The process perspective provides a positive view of life and change. The thing-oriented mind frequently experiences everything as less than ideal, because everything is less than perfect. In contrast, the process-focused mind sees things as part of a pattern of growth in which one can see and appreciate trends. In a case where process is trending negatively, one may sense that adjustments are needed, rather than seeing the unwanted current result as a disaster. To use the highway example again, we observe the process of driving as it moves us toward a desired destination. Road signs showing we have made an incorrect turn are not calamities, but merely indicators that a change of process is required. But haven't we all known someone who—without understanding life as a continuing flow, a changing and changeable process—because of a "missed turn" in life, became distraught and perhaps even self-destructive? With a positive world view, one maintains energy to improve the process and only occasionally checks the milestones to measure progress. The focus is always on the process. When we focus on things, we want to make progress toward achieving them, but we do not know how.

Alan: Then there really are no "end points" in any process. All "endings" are merely shifts or transformations. An engine does not "end" when it is shipped from the factory; it is now just beginning its intended work. When scrapped, it begins its deterioration process. If it is true that there are no end points, neither are there any beginning points. The engine as "thing" is an isolated part of its ongoing process.

Tom: That's correct. And we humans are also in process. However, our content orientation to the world fragments and disconnects us from others and from ourselves. We make clocks to measure our day so we know the hour when it ends. We shut off and turn on different pieces of content the same way we change channels on our television set. We compare the results of our lives—income, title and position, possessions, honors—with those of others to see who is better. We judge the various contents in the world and miss the connections between processes that create the whole.

Alan: Content/thing is "what." Content/thing is knowledge. Content/thing is fixed images. Content/thing is distinction, discrimination, differentiation. Content/thing is scores or grades and winners or losers. Content/thing is answers. Content/thing is right ways. Content/thing is style. We fill our heads with content/things all the time. They shape our lives and filter what we allow ourselves to see. What we get is a distorted and partial view of ourselves and the world.

Tom: Conversely, process is "how." It presents itself to us when we let go of all the content. Our appropriate response to what is going on around and within us all the time is sensing and learning and appreciating. There is a saying, "If you want to be the best, focus on doing your best, not on how you compare to others." We have heard it, or something like it, over and over, but still we focus on goals and ends rather than on our own processes and capabilities. The current rage of benchmarking coming out of the Malcolm Baldridge competitions is only a recent example of this focus.

Alan: Do you see no value in benchmarking?

Tom: There is value in seeing how well an excellent company focuses on, and carries out, processes similar to the ones we are engaged in. It ceases to be valuable when people look at the content of what's happening and go back home to copy the content. By doing so, they ignore their own capability, their own context, and their creative abilities to become the organization that others want to benchmark against.

Alan: In other words, that application of benchmarking is just another example of content/thing thinking?

Tom: Exactly.

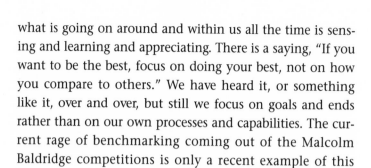 ***Exercise in Process vs Thing Focus:*** Next time you are watching television, select a commercial to watch. Do not focus on what they are selling, but on how. What is unfolding in the main "story" of the commercial? What is the process trying to do besides sell you a product? What are the implied messages? What conditioning do they seem to be aiming at? Notice if you are being drawn to the content and watch your own process as that happens. What triggered the switch? Do this several times until you can just watch the process throughout the entire commercial without being "caught" by the product.

CHAPTER 15

The Process of Now

Tom: "Process" has become an overused and often misunderstood word. For most people, process means the cause/effect flow of events, as in the Mideast Peace Process. This is a useful and not inaccurate definition, but it misses an aspect of process critical to quality consciousness. That aspect refers to the way things are being done in the moment (I'm using "moment" in the sense of "instantaneous"). In any one moment there cannot be related cause and effect. There are both causes and effects in a given moment but they are not the cause and effect of each other: the effects are from some prior cause and the causes are of some future effects. Since the moment is instantaneous, it cannot have the before-and-after sequence we apply to cause/effect because the elapsed time is essentially zero. The process of now is a singular event, awareness of which consists only and entirely of attention to the here and now. Often we call this way of being "presence." To be fully present with something or someone is to transcend cause and effect.

Almost none of us is ever fully present at our workplace—or anywhere else, for that matter. We are conditioned to look behind us for the real or imagined causes of actions, or in front of us to discover or predict how certain effects will play out. Because of this conditioning, we believe we can rather easily and straightforwardly create other causes to achieve new effects.

To be present with an organization is to realize that the cause/effect phenomenon is bewilderingly complex, once we get beyond the purely mechanical level. On the mechanical level, drilling a hole in metal is a simple cause/effect operation. It takes place on what we may call the surface of being where, as comedian Flip Wilson used to say, "what you see is what you get." On deeper levels, where there are complex interactions between forces and individuals, there is no such direct cause/effect relationship.

When we treat events in organizations as simple cause/effect phenomena we miss the deeper workings of what is actually going on. Humans at work or in any kind of social setting are involved in a kind of interconnected dance, where we are at once both cause and effect. The surface events we pay so much attention to are moved by deeper patterns and rhythms that occur in longer time cycles and thus are harder to perceive. Lasting social or organizational changes result from underlying cultural shifts that are difficult to detect, and even more difficult to influence.

The way to notice cultural shifts is to plunge into the cultural ocean depths and stop watching the surface ripples. But given the short-term orientation of most business organizations in the U.S., such a plunge is very difficult to take. Leaders are always under tremendous pressure to "do something now" to respond to the surface ripples. The cause/effect illusions created by these ripples on the surface of organizational life stimulate but also capture us, so that we remain unaware of the subtle, deep forces responsible for major shifts. And when things seem to get better as a result of our frantic activities, we think we have caused the improvements to happen. Unfortunately, these better results almost always get worse over time, because the deep forces—the dynamic systems—override them.

Sensing an organization accurately requires us to be present with it for a while, noting but not being fooled by the ripples. Similarly, to notice the process of now of a team of people is to go beneath the issues and words rippling around the room. To notice the process of now within ourselves is to go beneath our emotional reactions to observe how the center is moving in response to deeper currents.

Alan: Even in the physical world of quality we know that to adjust each variation (or ripple) in a machine's output throws it out of control. We should instead collect enough data to sense the movement of the overall process. Statistical process measurement is a mechanical way to be with the machine in the process of the now. That is relatively easy to do.

But I know from experience that it is extremely difficult to stay with the now of my own being. I am easily knocked off balance by the cause/effect whirlabout dance I'm in. Within myself are different drives and urges, all trying to gain control and cause certain desired effects.

Tom: That's certainly so. But the notion that some part of us causes us to be what we are is an illusion. A ripple on the surface is not the ocean moving. A momentary emotion is not our core being. Like the weather in Chicago, our emotions change quickly. To bounce around on the surface level is to have no peace. Worse, it sustains the illusion that we are irresistibly driven by cause and effect. (You insult me and I'll insult you or feel hurt). If we never stand still in the ups and downs of our lives we will never see our constant depths of being beneath the ripples.

Alan: I understand that one of the important reasons why Zen practitioners meditate and practice just sitting and breathing is to bring their dancing, whirling selves to a standstill so they might have a chance to see what's beneath the surface.

Tom: Yes, and in the often frantic world of business it is very difficult to quiet ourselves down in that way. But it is essential if we are to gain clarity about ourselves and about what's really going on around us.

Comments and Reflections: Here's an opportunity to check your own mental "pulse." How do you slow yourself down and become still? If you find it difficult or impossible to do that, what do you tell yourself to keep from doing it? _____

_____

_____

_____

_____

_____

_____

_____

_____

CHAPTER 16

Critical Characteristics of Kaizen Management

Tom: The capability of an organization to move from crisis-driven to kaizen-driven is highly contingent upon its ability to move along two intersecting axes. One movement is from non-systemic to highly systemic, and the other is from high to low judgmentalism. Continuous improvement depends on increasing capability on both axes. The direction of movement is shown by the arrow in the following diagram.

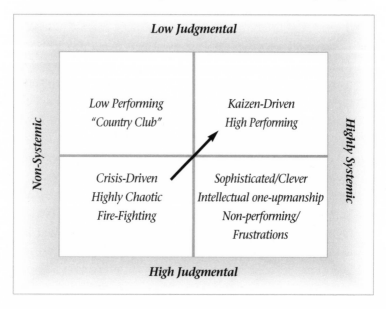

It is often difficult for crisis-driven people to think in terms of both/and. Extreme crisis-driven thinking invariably sees issues as if they were sharply separated into either/or. To understand the model above, we need always to keep both systemic and low-judgmental thinking in mind. Please remember that this is not a judgmental, but a descriptive model. It is a tool for taking stock of how things work or don't work, and where to look for understanding.

Here is what the axes represent:

Low-High Judgmentalism is a continuum that describes how strongly people view all aspects of the workplace from within a right/wrong framework. The highly judgmental have clear ideas of how things should be, and have strong blaming or faultfinding reactions when their world or work does not conform to those ideas. The ego's need to be right creates these strong reactions.

On the other end, those with low judgmentalism also have clear ideas of desired performance of the work, but their reactions are not to blame or find fault. Instead they accept what is, and maintain a positive and supportive attitude toward improvement and change. Those who don't need to find fault view things from a neutral stance and are willing to start with the existing situation. The highly critical are always making okay-ness a precondition, and therefore are almost never where the situation actually is. They either believe everything is a disaster and are frantically busy trying to patch everything, or they view these efforts with cynical contempt. This attitude stems from knowing that they will not really be able to correct anything in such an incompetent operation.

The low-systemic view treats the world as a series of events separated from each other in time and space. Causal relationships are narrow and linear, if they exist at all. Moreover, the low-systemic approach treats the issue at hand as a unique event, one that has never happened before and will never happen again. Obviously this approach is accurate to some extent, since every event is unique in some way. However, this extreme differentiation makes us incapable of seeing patterns and similarities between issues and events, as well as blocking our perception of the interconnectedness of all things.

On the other hand, the high-systemic view sees the interconnection between elements of various parts of the work system. Relatedness over time and space form a picture of how things operate. Multiple cause/effect relationships and patterns are observed and connected to outcomes. This view has a capacity for handling complexity without becoming overwhelmed and confused. To maintain clarity in the midst of complexity requires both analytical and intuitive/holistic mental processes. Over time, various patterns of operation are observed, and are fine-tuned by the blending of critical factors.

Here is how the combinations work:

In the low-system, high-judgmentalism quadrant one finds a classic crisis-driven person who is ready to take on anything that comes his or her way. People show up at work to find out what is "hot" for that day. Much of the action is taken with a sigh of contempt and anger at those others (bosses, customers, suppliers, staffs, etc.) who are messing up and making life difficult for them. There are a lot of victims in this quadrant who feel no one cares about them and their work, and who, in turn, don't care about others' work. It's a highly competitive, every-person-for-himself-or-herself, survival-of-the-fittest, put-them-down-before-they-put-you-down kind of workplace. Obviously this description is exaggerated for effect and contrast, but the tendency is plain and familiar.

A low-system, low-judgmentalism workplace has many of the hectic patterns of the classic crisis-driven situation, but not the strongly negative attitude. People get along well, communicate well, support each other, and sincerely care. They usually don't see their connection to customers' needs and pain, suppliers' problems, or any other issues outside their circle of close associates. They are an insulated and isolated "happy family." Many performance issues are not raised because it would create conflict and disruption. The highest value in this operation is comfort. It is a "country club" atmosphere.

People in the high-judgmentalism, high-systemic arena are tough to deal with because they have "good" and highly sophisticated answers to performance problems. Clear connections are made to the customer, marketplace, supply base, etc., but requests for improved performance are invariably made with veiled threats. Overblown and expensive technologies are proposed to replace incompetent people; highly theoretical statements are made about how things should be, and especially how people should be. One-upmanship is commonplace. The self is usually not examined as part of the system, mainly because it is too painful and risky to expose the self to the clever, sophisticated "slings and arrows" of the many critics. Change is difficult because there are too many new, good ideas abounding, and people are too busy judging the rightness or wrongness of those ideas to actually try them out.

The high-systemic, low-judgmentalism operation is Kaizen-driven, striving for collective and continuous improvement. The system is seen as an integrated whole so appropriate improvements can be made. When experiments in improvement are tried, there is a sense of support and excitement. Inevitable mistakes do not create panic and retreat through fear of punishment. Rather, a search for deeper understanding of what went wrong leads to increased confidence that the next time it will work better. Constant renewal of effort is accompanied by new insights, which are widely shared. Operations that don't work well are examined closely with an eye to improvement. New ideas are welcomed and integrated into previous learnings, rather than judged good or bad. When ideas are not appropriate, it is a question of fit or timing rather than of right or wrong.

In most large organizations, we find each of the described quadrants represented. Individuals within a department may be in different quadrants. This diagnostic tool may be used to assess how we currently work and where opportunities exist to shift toward the high-system, low-judgmentalism quadrant. And of course the same tool may be used to look at ourselves.

 Exercise: Reflect for a few moments on your work environment in the light of the four subcultures described above. Do you see any resemblances? If so, which ones do you recognize? Which is dominant? Are you deeply satisfied with this environment? From your standpoint, could it be better?

What might you do to make it better—that is, less judgmental and more systemic?

If the environment is highly judgmental, what part do you play in keeping it that way? (This question asks you to be self-observing, not self-judgmental.) If it is low-systemic, how do you participate in maintaining that orientation? (Again, simply note, and withhold self-blame.) How might you begin to move in the direction of low-judgmental/high systemic? (Remember, the higher your position in your department or company, the more influential your behavior will be. But even a person of low hierarchical status influences others if they see that changed behavior is beneficial.)

Now think of your family system. Where do you as a family fit in this matrix? Go through the same thought process as above. Then go through the same process with yourself in relation to yourself.

CHAPTER 17

Reflective Thinking

[E-Mail message from Tom to Alan]
Alan, here's another little article that came out of my reflections on
a consultation I did the other day. Thought you'd be interested.—Tom.

Kaizen requires that we think reflectively. Reflective thinking is simply the ability to see issues below their concrete and physical manifestations, recognizing that actions or data are symptoms of some underlying phenomenon or pattern.

As mentioned before, most of us are trained to react to a specific event or action confronting us. In certain circumstances that reaction is all that is required, but in order truly to understand a system we must be able to use the concrete to reflect back onto the larger system. Without this ability, we are doomed to react endlessly to the events and actions that constantly bombard us. At best we only hold our own, never able to take charge of our lives or our work.

A case in point might be an outbreak of carpal tunnel syndrome on a production line. Typically, both victims and managers will take specific actions to remedy the situation. The victim will seek medical advice and treatment; the manager will see what can be done about changing the wrist motions required to do the job, or rotate operators from job to job to provide relief from the strain. On at least one occasion I know of, the carpal tunnel syndrome was an indirect result of a piecework incentive system that challenged workers to produce twice as many parts as the quota called for in order to earn about twice their usual daily rate. As long as the incentive system was in place, carpal tunnel syndrome continued to plague workers and managers, but no one could see the connection between the system and the disability. In fact, the managers started to blame the workers for conspiring with their doctors to get disability pay.

Also on the production floor, statistics help us think reflectively. When mass producing any item, we must use statistics to reveal a machine's capability, since we cannot see it directly. Instead, what we can see are those critical measurements of a product that reflect the processes the machine has just performed. Each individual product is less important than the trend successive measurements reveal. We look for those trends to tell us when the machine runs out of tolerance. The parts produced are really only results of the machine's operating process, which is what we care about.

It is worth re-emphasizing that reflective statistical thinking is concerned with the collective pattern revealed by many parts, not with the "goodness" or "badness" of any individual part. Unfortunately, most people are taught to look at each individual part and judge it as "good" or "reject." This crisis-driven mentality makes it impossible to understand the importance or usefulness of statistical data gathering.

At higher organizational levels the need for reflective thinking also holds true. Too often managers are quick to react to an event as unique, rather than to ask whether this is part of a pattern that reveals a malfunctioning system. Labor-management communications are wasted on continual bickering over individual grievances when data could be compiled to identify trends or patterns and gain insight into how the organization's systems might negatively affect people's morale or working conditions.

Incidents that proceed from larger systems follow patterns. Studying these patterns can lead us to see flaws in the overall design. Behind that design we may discern the concepts and beliefs governing how we run our business. To get to this deeper insight requires a great deal of reflective thinking. Too often we executives are trained and rewarded, not for reflecting, but for our ability to react quickly with snap decisions. We pride ourselves on quick judgments but do not dig into the deeper causes of problems whose elimination might lead the organization to significant improvement.

The ability to think reflectively is also a powerful tool for personal growth. Reflective thinking does not cast judgments, divide things up into their component parts, and evaluate. It is not analytical thinking. It is more a process of looking at an event or entity as a whole. When we reflect on ourselves, we notice our patterns of operating in the world. We observe and think about the images and concepts that may lie behind and frame those patterns. This process allows us to see our deeper selves, not to judge, but simply to regard ourselves as "who we are." The trick here is not to become a crisis-driven critic partway through the process, switching from simple reflection on ourselves to judgment on what is revealed. Whether or not we like what we find, we tend to pay more attention to our judgment than to a simple awareness of who we are.

[E-Mail back to Tom]

Tom, you have taught me that to approach issues reflectively is not to react quickly to them, but to wait quietly and see what the actions and circumstances reveal about the underlying systems in play. Over time, patterns are discernible and changes can be made in the systems. Your article gets at these points very well. Thanks.

Comments and Reflections _____

_____

_____

_____

_____

_____

CHAPTER 18

New Mental
Frameworks

[One evening after consulting with a struggling company]

Alan: Whew! that was a rough day. I don't think we persuaded those guys that, by insisting on laying down rules, enforcing them, and telling the workers that their role is to do what they're told, they're shooting themselves in the foot. The workers sure aren't buying it.

Tom: I'm afraid you're right. In order to compete successfully in the business world of the future, managers and workers alike will have to change dramatically the mental framework through which they see and interpret the workplace. And this was a perfect, though sad, case in point.

Alan: As I recall, by "mental framework" you mean the basic assumptions, organizing structures, principles and premises that our minds create to make sense out of the apparent chaos and randomness of events that we see swirling about us. What change do you think these clients have to make?

Tom: From their current framework of "work as a machine," to "work as a process."

Alan: I think I understand work as a process. That refers to how work is performed. But what do you mean by "work as a machine"?

Tom: First of all, let's be clear. There is no moral tone to either of these frameworks, since both may be used by people to help or harm the world and humankind. I am not talking about values or ideology, by which I mean some "right belief." The change is required simply because to see work as process is to become more efficient and effective.

Let's go back a bit in time. We in the West (Europe and its cultural descendants) have been trained in the Cartesian and Newtonian mental framework. This framework trains us to see the universe as a giant machine controlled by laws created, and in turn obeyed, by Divine Mind. Under its influence, men like James Watt created the Industrial Revolution in which mechanisms—steam engines, gears, and levers—dominated the scene, controlled by intelligent human masters who stood apart from their mechanical creatures.

Although our tools and technology, and the science on which they are based, have changed dramatically, our mental constructs have not. Most of us build or support organizations based on this outmoded mechanical model. We assume that those who lead and manage are in control and are not themselves integral parts of the organizational "machine."

Alan: Okay, so when you say "work as machine," you mean an organizational machine where work is performed by willing workers, with managers standing behind and above them, telling them what to do and seeing that they do it. A common saying that illustrates this mental framework is, "So-and-so runs the company." A machine is something you run. But if more recent developments in science and technology have eclipsed the Newtonian framework, why does it still seem to function that way?

Tom: Because that approach has worked successfully for almost two hundred years and has established thought patterns and behaviors—habits if you will—that are still with us. The patterns were powerful, because it was generally believed that they were in tune with nature, which in some ways they are. However, we now know that the Cartesian-Newtonian worldview is seriously limited—that there are other, much more powerful frameworks that take in and explain much more data. That is why we need to re-examine our mental frameworks, just as Einstein reframed Newtonian physics in the light of new experimental and observational evidence. When he did, he came to a new, more powerful understanding of how the universe works.

Alan: So you're not saying that Newton was wrong and Einstein was right, but just that Einstein had a better understanding of how everything works. Similarly, the kind of mental framework that sees work as process is a better way of understanding how work can be more effectively performed. For example, the machine notion suggests that managers must control people and things; but from what I read in contemporary scientific literature, systems are self-managing—and so are people when they have the direction, support, and resources they need.

Tom: That's it. I've drawn up a table that contains some central assumptions of "machine thinking" about work, which I have listed in the left-hand column. To embrace the new, "process" thinking, we must first recognize our current patterns. We usually assume these patterns reflect reality, and we can never really challenge them until we become conscious of them and ask, why these, rather than others?

Alan: Like the "givens" in geometry.

Tom: Exactly, except the givens I'm talking about are not conscious. Note that if you substitute "machine" for "organization" in this list, you will see that they are interchangeable.

There are probably more elements, but these should be enough to get a picture of the mental framework commonly used to create our organizations. Obviously, trying to make a human organization operate according to mechanistic structures has definite and costly limitations. The chief advantages cited by leaders and managers of thinking and structuring this way are those of predictability and control. But do such advantages really exist? Anyone who has spent time in large organizations—or even in small ones—knows that crises can occur at any moment, no matter how ironclad the structure. Pursuit of control and predictability leads not to machine-like efficiency and smooth operation, but to their opposites. We are much better advised to develop systemic structures based on freedom—or, as you called it, self-management—and probability, than on control and predictability.

As I've just suggested, a "process thinking" orientation is one based on a worldview that sees probabilities rather than certainties, responsible freedom rather than control, as the best approximations of the way nature works. Freedom in this orientation is based on the responsibility individuals feel to advance the overall good of the larger unit, such as the company, in innovative and creative ways. I've listed some of the thought processes critical to this thinking in the following table.

Again, there are probably more elements in this type of thinking. People thinking this way are more likely to move their organizations to ever-higher levels of performance, because of their positive view of the nature of humans—that the vast majority are intelligent, responsible, trustworthy, and want to do their best. A negative view creates a highly controlled, mechanistic style of thinking. Thinking frameworks lead to the kinds of organizations we create and the kinds of behaviors we expect.

In summary, this table suggests a change to something radically different from anything we have attempted before. The very heart of our logic systems must change. To make this change requires managers to actively desire to become aware of and alter current thought processes, rather than just the organizational forms these processes have created. Such changes require us to know ourselves on

Standards of Performance

Logic: Organizations are designed to perform at certain capacity levels when operating as designed. Leads to next point.

Advantages: Success is easily determined. Predictability is dominant to ensure smooth flow. One knows when things are "right."

Issues: Eliminates individual creativity for improvements. Hitting standard becomes an end point. Standard is the best obtainable within a fixed framework.

Variance Watching

Logic: Role of people is to make sure organization is hitting standard. Main activity is to fix variances from standard.

Advantages: Takes little personal energy to critique. Problems come to the observer who then reacts.

Issues: People get vested in firefighting and resist really making the organization run to standard.

Functional Orientation

Logic: Each piece is designed separately and can be attached to the organization to upgrade the total system (much like attaching new fuel systems to an old engine.)

Advantages: Requires little over-all knowledge of the system. Allows specialists to become highly proficient in small pieces of the operation.

Issues: Creates cross-functional friction and confusion of desired effects. Does not "fit" into total system and creates systemic variances frequently not the ones desired.

a much deeper level and to support and engage others in doing the same. Moreover, it requires that each of us chooses between freedom and security. To choose freedom is to remove the boundaries we have set around ourselves and our organizations, opening us up to face an uncertain future together. The choice of security in the familiar and the known is the choice of certain stag-

Linear Thinking

Logic: Depicts the organization as series of causes and effects driven from various fragments of the operation.

Advantages: High predictability short-range issues that can be isolated from overall operation.

Issues: Ignores too many other impacts constantly being made on the organization. Creates tunnel vision, relocates problems elsewhere.

Friction Resolution

Logic: All organizations have normal friction due to different objectives of parts. Needs to be "well lubricated" to work well by smoothing friction.

Advantages: Organizations run at some level of performance long after they normally would grind to a halt.

Issues: Highly expensive coordinators, referees, special program managers, etc., add heavily to costs of production. Personnel develop vested interest in being an "oiler."

Motivation Factors

Logic: Movement is based on external addition of fuel (money, status, or power) to keep the operation accelerating.

Advantages: Develops highly driven parts and individuals who get supercharged.

Issues: Becomes very expensive to buy more performance when much of the fuel goes toward overcoming hyper-friction.

nation and degeneration—not to mention the fact that when we choose security we delude ourselves, because it does not exist.

Alan: I want to study these lists further. Right now, though, I'm making this connection. Recently I read that natural evolution takes place through three processes: chance; survival of

PROCESS THINKING

Standardize/Kaizen
Logic: Organizations are capable of performing in ways not yet understood. The operation is in constant evolution.
Advantages: Taps into creativity and innovation by unleashing the capability of individuals to improve.
Issues: Demands a higher level of mental energy on the part of people. We never get done.

Opportunity Awareness
Logic: Organizations improve best when people constantly look for improvements in individual, group, and system performance.
Advantages: Changes outlook from negative problem solving to positive exploitation of opportunities on a large-scale basis.
Issues: People lose the security of being knowledgeable of the current system.

Holistic Approach
Logic: Organizations are in a dynamic state of change from many directions. The piece is always understood in the context of a larger whole.
Advantages: People begin making decisions and acting from a view that looks beyond functional boundaries and personal ego needs.
Issues: Specialists and even functional generalists must broaden their base of action and understanding.

the fittest (which does not mean the strongest and most competitive, but those who learn best how to cooperate with and adapt to their environment); and free choice. We have already said that accidents or chance occurrences happen and can wreck the best laid plans. Now you seem to be saying that the assumptions we have been taught to make, about how organizations must be run in order to provide us with a secure future, no longer work very well. We have also made other assumptions about what human beings are like. These assumptions have given rise to organizational systems

Interactive Flows

Logic: Organization becomes adapted to facilitating the movement of products and services that must interact in a supportive manner.

Advantages: People see connectedness to larger process and determine more appropriate fits. Self-orienting rather than coordinated by others.

Issues: Specialists and even functional generalists must broaden their base of action and understanding.

Moved by Will

Logic: Organizations are driven by the combined will of individual performers aligned with common vision. Money rewards performance to that end.

Advantages: Energy is escalated by belonging to a high-performance unit. Feeling of responsible power creates freedom to perform.

Issues: Seniority security is removed that allows the individual to stop learning and moving. Initiative and effort are rewarded. Leadership provides worthy purpose and vision to align with and model new behaviors.

and structures that are shaky, too. So these "security-providing" assumptions must all undergo radical change to become more aligned with how we are beginning to understand the way change works in nature. To make us better adapted, new systems and structures will have to be invented that are aligned with these new understandings. We can choose to make the necessary changes and learn to cooperate in new ways. By doing so, we will have a better chance of surviving, but there are no guarantees. In either case, if we're after security, forget it. However, if organizationally we choose to retain our old assumptions and ways of thinking, we're certain to degenerate and eventually become extinct. Is that it?

Tom: That's it.

Alan: Hmm. No control, no predictability, no security. What's left?

Tom: Creativity, responsible freedom, and each other as partners working in harmony, plus an understanding that we are more closely aligned with the way the universe itself works. To me, that's a joyful prospect.

Comments and Reflections

_____

_____

_____

_____

_____

_____

_____

_____

CHAPTER 19

Business Thinking

[E-Mail from Tom to Alan]
Alan, another thought. Share it around as you see fit. —Tom.

As business managers we tend to believe that our thinking processes are sufficient to comprehend and give direction and clarity to our organizations. In studying the Japanese and working with a wide variety of U.S. managers, I have observed that there are some generic thought processes in each of the two cultures that underlie most of their approaches. But they are not the same. By itself, each culture's approach reflects only a partial picture of the whole of business enterprise. Thus each lacks balance and completeness. Taken together, however, they create a comprehensive approach.

		Scope	
		Holistic	*Fragmented*
Focus of Attention	*External*	*Strategic Planning*	*Strategic Goal Setting*
	Internal	*Capability Design*	*Capability Action*

In the previous diagram I have identified four approaches, each of which is important for comprehensive and effective management.

Across the top we have the scope of the thinking process, holistic on the left and fragmented on the right. A holistic, comprehensive view takes in all of the critical elements of the situation being viewed. A narrow, fragmented focus, on the other hand, looks at only one thing at a time in a sequential, serial, or functional way. This view may or may not fit within the context of the whole.

On the vertical axis we have an internal and external focus of attention. The external notices things or elements apparently separate from and outside the physical boundaries of the observer's organization. Examples would be the market, competitors, national economic trends, etc. The internal focus looks inward to the organization's operational characteristics. It is a reflective or introspective view of what the organization is about, how the operations actually work.

Combining the two sets, we have the essence of strategic planning, strategic goal setting, operational design, and operational action. Defining each one gives us some insights into managerial differences and blindspots.

Strategic Planning. This arena looks at the global economic, market, financial, competitive, regulatory issues that face a large business. Capability in this area is determined by the number of issues one can comprehend, and clarity about how they interact. Strategic planning positions a company for new products, new markets, new governmental actions and regulations, policy decisions.

Strategic Goal Setting. This arena deals with the process of translating the broad direction of planning into specific goals and objectives that need to be pursued in order to be successful in the future marketplace. These are specific descriptions of what the various products or services we offer the market should look like, that is, price, performance, quality, durability, reliability, availability, etc. Strategic goal setting focuses on what we want to introduce into the economy in the way of desirable products and services.

Capability Design. This third arena is concerned with the whole organization's actual operation. How do the various processes and systems come together to produce a product or service? At the plant level, it is the overall master plan that covers technology, material, workers, facilities, information, measures, management, and product. Capability design is a holistic creation of internal operation.

Capability Action. This last arena focuses on the various internal measures of separate elements of the actual operation: cost per piece, labor grievances, quality rejects, tardiness and absenteeism, defects, and so on. These activities may or may not be understood in the context of the overall design. Capability action is the actual situation encountered daily by most workers.

In studying U.S. and Japanese companies, I have noticed that most U.S. managers tend to value the strategic portions, while most Japanese tend to value the capability portions. We have elaborate worldwide strategic plans and goals and cannot understand the general Japanese slowness to respond to market opportunities. On the other hand, typical Japanese managers constantly work on developing and training employees and improving operations with kaizen, and cannot understand why in the U.S. we are so inefficient and operationally inept. The best companies in both cultures practice very well in all four arenas.

A company that is only strategic sets high goals that it cannot implement because no one understands or works on the capability design. It promises more than it can deliver. A company that concentrates only on capability may make an extremely good product for a nonexistent market.

Part of the difficulty in switching from a strategic focus to a capability focus is the reflective thinking required for the latter, and the negative consequences that often follow its omission. For example, to determine why deliveries cannot be made on time, one may have to reflect backwards through the entire delivery process—perhaps even beyond that—to find the breakdown. This reflective process can feel very threatening to managers if they believe that an open analysis of operations for purposes of improvement will be seen by upper management as revealing evidence of incompetence or malpractice. If investigation leads to punishment, managers will quickly lose the desire to reflect on operations and look for other ways to improve, ways removed from their own areas of responsibility.

American business operations need to see the value of balancing and appreciating all of these thinking approaches. For us in the United States, the biggest gap in understanding is our inability to see the overall capability of an organization. Without clear perception of the total internal system, we may fix fragments, but will not improve the whole. A fragmented intervention may make things better for a short while, but over the longer term it simply causes the system to oscillate for a while before it settles back into the same old pattern.

Comments and Reflections

CHAPTER 20

Strategic Thinking vs Capability Thinking

[E-Mail from Tom]

Alan, I'm on a roll! Here's a follow-up article I wrote on the two kinds of thinking required for effectiveness, whether business or personal. It represents a refinement of the conversation you and I had about business thinking. You might want to pass it around as a kind of sequel if you like it.—Tom.

In order to perform well in the world, a person, organization, industry, or even a nation must do good strategic thinking and good capability thinking. This observation may seem obvious, but we find that they are not given equal and balanced consideration. Strategic thinking may be summarized as what needs to be done. The strategists in World War II, for example, decided that what the Allies needed to do to defeat Germany was to open a three-front offensive from the south, west, and east.

Capability thinking has to do with how and depends not only on the way something must be done, but also on the skills, resources, logistics, and other requirements needed to carry it out. Thus, in the same World War II example, the Allies had to be sure they had the matériel, trained and combat-ready troops, supply lines, air support, transportation, and all the other necessities to carry out a successful three-front war.

Strategic Thinking.

Most strategic thinking is based on an analysis of what would be an appropriate or successful use of current or potential resources. This thinking is carried on within the overall purpose the organization is seeking to pursue. "Success" or "failure" or "appropriateness" is defined in terms of its overall purpose.

To illustrate in business terms, a company will make different strategic decisions about what products to make or what markets to supply, depending on its purpose. Maximum short-term profitability will drive a strategy different from that of long-term customer satisfaction.

On the personal level, an egocentric purpose, like seeking personal power over others, drives strategies different from those of a purpose aimed at being more effective in service to others. Because it involves one's whole being, I call the latter a systemic purpose.

Strategic thinking begins with a purpose, whether conscious or unconscious, and lays out a plan to enable the organization to achieve it. This process looks outward, taking in key environmental data—needs, kinds of customers, technology, etc.—and identifying a market for the organization's or person's product or service. A typical example is the way most of us planned our careers in high school or college. We looked outward to see what was available or needed, and tried to decide what we should become in order to "sell" ourselves and be successful in society's eyes. Key aspects of strategic thinking, then, are outward focus, analytical approach, and connection with purpose.

Capability Thinking.

Obviously connected with the question of what needs to be done is the issue of how to do it. It is easy to say we want to be a doctor, but the how requires years of hard work. It takes great dedication, a combination of will and spirit, to pursue a medical career. Similarly, without the will and spirit to do what it takes to achieve its purpose, no company ever achieves its strategic goals or purpose. Simply having the will, spirit, commitment, and dedication, however, is not enough. And here is where capability thinking plays its part.

Capability thinking is an inward appraisal or diagnosis. It focuses on what the members of an organization—or we personally—know how to do, and what the next steps of development of that knowhow need to be in order to progress toward our purpose. Capability thinking tends to be more real-time than the abstract, analytical time of strategic thinking. We grow capability continuously through moment-to-moment action, i.e., learning takes place concurrently with doing. For example, if we intend to become doctors we may do a lot of preparatory learning, but we become doctors only as we actually practice medicine—first as interns, then as residents, and finally as full-fledged practitioners.

A positive will and spirit allows an organization or person to look at itself honestly, try new things, and continue the development process. A negative or absent will and spirit, whether in organizations or individuals, will avoid looking honestly at itself, and instead only pretend to be healthy and growing. Positive will and spirit sees problems as areas of potential improvement and the next opportunity for learning and growth. Diagnoses are used constantly to upgrade the ability of the company or person to do work more effectively. Then strategic planning aims that ability at some external goal. The key aspects of capability are inward focus, honest diagnosis, and active approach, all arising from positive will and spirit.

Operational Issues.

Effectiveness, either personal or organizational, is an ability to do both strategic and capability thinking, to know the difference, and to know when each is appropriate. As I have observed, we in the West tend to emphasize strategic thinking, while the Japanese tend to emphasize capability thinking. Many U.S. companies have great plans to do things, and lag in their ability to implement. The Japanese, on the other hand, have implemented excellent work improvements but historically have lagged in strategic planning for new products. The world's best companies do both well. The West's tendency to start with an outward focus is based on our philosophical/religious heritage which has taught us to look outside ourselves for the meaning of life and being. The opposite philosophical/religious orientation is prevalent in Asia. But these are only starting points and do not prevent any of us from doing both.

Unfortunately, we are too comfortable, both individually and organizationally, with the style of thinking we grew up with. Strategists forget to build capability, and capability thinkers forget their purpose. For individuals, overemphasizing a strategic life can lead to great material wealth, but also a sense of emptiness or futility. Overemphasizing capability can lead to great personal learning, but no contribution to the society at large. Balance and harmony between the two is the key to effectiveness.

Companies face the same struggle. An ambitious strategic plan can deaden the will and spirit if capability is neglected. Overemphasizing capability with poor strategic direction can leave the business in a competitive deadend, as great buggy whip manufacturers learned to their sorrow.

In summary, both strategic and capability thinking are critical to long-term survival. Long-term viability always begins with short-term actions, from which we learn if we reflect on them and on the results they create. The danger we face in the United States is that of overdoing strategic and underdoing capability thinking. When working on capability, which has to do with what we are able to do right now, we must be careful not to slip into strategic thinking, which has to to with what we would like to be able to do, or even seriously intend to do. Describing future needs or intentions does not clarify where we are now; talking about goals is not the same as developing capability. Excellent leaders tie together the strategic vision, purpose, positive will and spirit, and capability of an ever-developing organization. With that balanced approach, they achieve excellence.

Comments and Reflections: Which type of thinking do you tend to emphasize? How might you strengthen your abilities in the other? _____

_____

_____

_____

_____

_____

_____

_____

_____

_____

CHAPTER 21

More on the Cause/Effect Illusion

Tom: As I have said before, we usually operate in a simple, linear, mechanical cause/effect way, believing that a problem is wholly caused by an immediately present agent and can be solved by taking action in direct response to this agent. Such a reactive and fragmented way of thinking drives us constantly to identify and blame the wrong agents for our numerous breakdowns. For example, we often accuse the person closest to a problem of being its perpetrator, or cut costs because our costs are "too high."

Alan: There are even times when we feel that somehow we must have been responsible, just because we were closest to something when it went wrong. But more commonly, we think the machine operator made the product poorly, the order taker made the wrong input to the system, the assembler was careless with a wrench or screwdriver.

Tom: Traditionally, in our hierarchical organizations we have found low-level people to be convenient scapegoats for an ineffective system. By focusing on the lowest level in a fragmented, simple cause/effect way, we managers have been able to proclaim our own innocence. And for this reason, most early "improvement efforts" are made on the shop floor, because "they" are the ones who need to be fixed. I am not saying that the shop floor does not need improvement, but my point is that by focusing only there we have failed to make much progress with improvement efforts.

A production system is an interrelated whole that contains a bewildering complexity of cause/effect relations. These relations are manifestations of powerful systems that underlie and therefore constitute "common causes" for many problems. The illusion that simple cause-and-effect is all there is blocks the way to deeper understanding of the systems that cause most of the problems we encounter. All of us tend to hold on to this illusion because we fear two results of looking deeper—that the "blame" will return to "fall on me," and that "I won't be smart enough to know what to do to control this complicated mess!"

Alan: I'd like to look at both fears in more detail.

Tom: Okay. Blaming and fault-finding comes from our need to be better or more worthy than others. Our compensation and evaluation systems support this comparative thinking, as do most of our cultural institutions: educational, athletic, and national. We find fault with others to make us feel "one up" or not as "one down." We think we improve our stature by diminishing that of others. Many people live a whole lifetime without learning that nothing is added to their stature by comparing themselves to others. Most of us do come to this realization eventually, usually accompanied by a great deal of pain at remembering the efforts we wasted on demonstrating our superiority.

Alan: Deborah Tannen, in her book *You Just Don't Understand,* has pointed to this tendency as a particularly male pattern in our culture. What about the second fear?

Tom: The second fear is based on our mistaken belief that somewhere out there someone knows how to predict accurately and control outcomes. The only thing all our planning and forecasting have ever demonstrated is how consistently inaccurate we are, and how events always take us by surprise. Nevertheless, when faced with a complex system that we don't (and can't) know, we feel out of control and inferior to those who, we are sure, do know. As we experience this fear of incompetence, we seek to simplify and explain, rather than "go with" the unknown to see if greater understanding will emerge. We would much rather suppress our fears by having an "answer" than have the system improve through our careful observation, letting the answer emerge out of the system's own working.

Alan: From my own experience, I can tell you that what we do is not consciously intended to mislead or deceive. Our response is automatic, the result of years of conditioning to have the "right answers" and to act as if we were in control when authorities ask the questions.

Tom: I know. But in reality, the only possible control is process control, control over how things happen, not over outcomes. It is based on a way of thinking that requires greater understanding and integration of systems.

At an early age most of us are conditioned to behave mechanically. In later years we may learn to be more unconditioned and thus more fully alive—what I have earlier called being present in the moment. Our conditioning is demonstrated every day by familiar phrases like, "He made me feel angry," or, "She hurt me with that remark." These phrases and many more are simple cause/effect mechanical statements. As long as we see ourselves as machines automatically reacting to outside stimuli, these statements seem to describe how we work.

Psychologists have made extensive studies of the typical patterns of cause/effect relationships in families and society. Because this research has found evidence of cause and effect, social scientists sincerely believe that this is the reality of being human. More recently some researchers have begun looking more deeply into family systems dynamics and have gained insight into the complex interworkings and influences of these systems on the family's individual members. But at the heart of all this research is still the assumption that humans are nothing more than conditioned, mechanical cause/effect beings. This behaviorist approach is useful: it improves the mechanical functioning of persons who are products of dysfunctional family systems. But is it the last word?

I believe that a unique characteristic of us humans is our capacity to act as free agents despite all the conditioning that has gone on in our early years. To be nonmechanistic is to be in a non-cause/effect relationship with others and the world, to be capable of making free choices and of creating something new.

As I've already pointed out, on the purely physical level, cause-and-effect still applies. For example, if you get hit by a car, the physical impact will be just the same as if you were simply a 150-pound slab of meat. But it is possible to be nonmechanistic in the mental or psychological aspects of our being.

A starting point for awareness of ourselves as free agents—and therefore responsible for our own lives—may be to see that all the causes of our mental or psychological pain are *our causes and our effects*. That is to say, we invent and own them; they belong to us.

Alan: You seem to be saying the same thing as the philosopher who observed, "Events are only events; it is our opinion of them that makes them either painful or pleasureful." I understand you to say that through some act of choice we make ourselves what we are. Our inner processes of thinking and our conditioned self-image come together to frame a conceptual world that is both the cause and the effect of our state of being. We invent all of it. No one makes us be anything; we ourselves choose. We choose to hold onto conceptions of the world that are the "cause" of all our disappointments, pain, pleasure, anger, frustrations, happiness. But you also suggest that this conceptual world, framed when we were very young, can be reframed to allow us to live more unconditionally and nonmechanistically—that is, to be more fully and uniquely human.

Tom: That's right. Having pointed to the possibility of an unfettered way of thinking, I still get questions from those whose framework of understanding remains the mechanical one of cause/effect. They ask, "How can I make this choice?" Translated this reads, "Tell me what to do (mechanism) for me to have the unconditioned state of being (effect)." One cannot become unmechanistic through mechanistic means. This is a great paradox, an apparent—but not an actual—contradiction.

Alan: I remember the first time I was confronted with this paradox. It was years before I met you, in a seminar in Madison, Wisconsin. I was furious at the young man who told me that my asking "how?" was itself part of a mental framework that was irrelevant to the one he was describing. I'm sure that at the time I would have accused him of making me angry. So I wouldn't be surprised if readers are tempted to throw this book against the wall now, if they haven't already!

Tom: I wouldn't either, but let me say a couple of things that might be helpful. Many people have walked this road, or one much like it, and it is useful to read their stories. Albert Einstein comes immediately to mind, as does St. Augustine. In their autobiographies both describe the sudden flashes or "explosions" of insight that caused them to see the world and themselves in entirely different ways. One moment it was this way, the next it was entirely different. Not that the data were different, they were simply configured or ordered differently according to different structures of meaning.

Another example of what I am talking about is the picture, which I'm sure you've seen, of the young woman looking at herself in a mirror. If you concentrate on the young woman, the picture stays just the same. But if you shift your focus slightly, suddenly it is no longer the picture of a young woman, but of a death's head or an old crone—I don't remember which right now. No matter how hard you try, you cannot see both the young woman and the old crone or death's head at the same time; you can see only one or the other. Now people can tell you that both pictures exist in the one picture—if you will, that is a mechanical "how to," as is the suggestion that you have to shift your focus. But they cannot tell you how to see the other picture: you either see it or you don't. Some people make the shift very quickly; others must contemplate the picture for hours. Some, perhaps, never see the other picture. But once they do see it, they wonder why they never saw it that way before, and it becomes very easy to shift back and forth quickly between the two pictures.

It is similar with this understanding that we create our own lives, that all the conditioning is a matter of choice, part of that same creation. If you don't see it immediately—and many don't—it might be helpful to read or hear others' stories; or it might be helpful just to sit and contemplate. Eventually the insight may come.

Exercise in contemplation: This reading suggests that not only are we capable of choosing freely and consciously what we *do* every day, we are also free to choose who we *are*. (Some of a spiritual or theological bent might argue that this choice must be made in conformity with who we really are in our essence—in other words, that this freedom of choice is conditioned to some extent, either by a karmic process or by divine inspiration or calling, i.e. vocation.) Many spiritual disciplines use mechanical means, such as chanting mantras or performing certain exercises or contemplating *Koans*, to lead practitioners to confront themselves with their nonmechanistic nature. But, as the reading claims, you cannot get to the nonmechanistic mechanically, and these disciplines agree. Even so, some leading of this kind can be helpful, if in no other way than to confront you with a blank wall without a door, a wall too high to climb over, too long to travel around, through which you must pass. With this preface, let's begin.

Be present to the everyday things you do as you are doing them. For example, as you are dressing, observe which leg you first put your underwear and trousers on (if you are a man), or how you put your dress on (if you are a woman), in what order you put on your socks or stockings (right or left foot first), shoes, and other articles of clothing. Notice your rituals as you eat or as you get ready to go to work. What comes in what order? Then notice what you are paying attention to as you drive to work, or as you ride or walk to work. Make either a mental or written note of your observations.

The following day, arise earlier than usual and, upon rising, choose to perform these habitual tasks differently. For example, if you habitually put your right sock or stocking on first, put the left one on first. Notice how it feels. It will probably feel awkward and somehow wrong. Continue that process of making conscious choices to override habits whenever you can remember to do so. (You might even try changing hands for writing—though we don't recommend that you try this in signing checks!) In every case, simply note the advantages of doing enormous numbers of things automatically and mechanically. But you can also change the way you do them through conscious choice.

After practicing these behavior changes for a few days, begin thinking about certain assumptions you make about yourself, and about who you are; for example, "I am no good at math," "I'm a bad person," "I don't have feelings," "I'm clumsy," or statements that begin, "I always" or "I never." Ask yourself where did I learn these? From whom? When? Under what circumstances? Are they useful to me now? How are they useful? What would be more useful? Who or what stops me from characterizing myself in these more useful ways? Can I imagine myself being this kind of person?

Don't be in a hurry to try to change things about yourself that you find you don't like. Just observe what those things are and live with the recognition for awhile. Every time you find yourself making some characterization, just be aware of it and ask, is it really true of me all the time or only part of the time? Most of us don't spend much time getting to know ourselves, but if we don't know who we are, how can we know what changes would be positive? That is what this exercise is all about.

CHAPTER 22

Work as Transforming, Not as Busy-ness

Tom: When I was in the army, my sergeant was always on my case. The reason was that I never looked busy. I often appeared to be taking a break or doing some non-work-related activity. When I was confronted, the dialogue would usually be something like this:

> *Sergeant: Why aren't you at your desk?*
> *Tom: Is someone waiting for me?*
> *Sergeant: No, but you're spending too much time away from your desk.*
> *Tom: Are my customers complaining?*
> *Sergeant: No. You know you have the best record of least customer complaints. I just think you're not busy enough.*
> *Tom: Oh, do you mean I need a larger workload? I already do a lot more than my peers.*
> *Sergeant: Well, not exactly. I just get upset when my people aren't busy.*
> *Tom: Sergeant, what do you want from me, a lot of busy-ness or high quality work?*

These "dialogues" made me a high-value pain in the neck to my sergeant.

The point of this story is that we have created managers who equate busy-ness with productivity. If one has ever worked at the bottom of an organization—and a lot of executives have not—it is easy to see where this attitude toward workers' activity leads. First, it creates a sense that "trying hard" is what counts. Working smart is downplayed or dismissed entirely, either because the boss doesn't want employees to look smarter or less hard-working than he or she, or because finding something else to do makes more work for the boss. The not-so-subtle message is, "keep busy at the things I tell you to be busy at."

Second, in the minds of most workers it becomes clear that minimal productivity is acceptable if you look busy. Substance becomes secondary to appearance. After a while the worker learns the rules of the game. While a compliant worker goes along, the non-compliant becomes stigmatized as a goof-off or troublemaker. This kind of worker thus justifies keeping supervisors around in the first place: they are necessary to keep workers in line and at their work.

Alan: Reflecting on your experience in the army, it appears likely to me that the greatest threat you posed to your supervisor was that he might come under criticism from his superiors for not finding enough for you to do. You were conscious of your customers' needs, responded to them with quality service, and because you were highly productive, you were the low-cost producer. Yet you were criticized because you didn't *look* busy. This strange insistence on busy-ness is almost universal, judging from the organizations I have been part of. Bosses need to see busy-ness. Even "results-oriented" supervisors are upset by people who produce without appearing to be busy. They seem to resent employees who "work smart."

Tom: "Working smart" simply entails seeing that the work we do is always a transformation of something relatively raw to something more finished as part of the total process. If we learn the work flow and then look at its critical elements, we can figure out easier and quicker ways to transform and still maintain quality. On the other hand, if we think work is activity—and we know that activity is what the boss really prizes—we will never figure out more efficient ways to transform the raw to finished. In such a situation, it's smart not to be smart.

Alan: One fruit of human civilization has been to decrease the time needed to make the products necessary for survival, thereby providing time for the mental activity required for higher development. Unfortunately, we have slipped back at times into thinking that extreme busy-ness in earning money is a badge of merit. In your story, the rewards—in this case, not being hassled by the supervisor—went to those who played the game according to the rules, not to those who could produce quality for the customer and have time and energy left over.

Tom: With some residue—like energy or money, that is, profit—we can invest in ourselves for new and greater accomplishments. When we use all our energy in busy-ness we are personally incurring a loss. We are spending down the capital, bankrupting our personal systems. This can easily be seen in the case of workaholics, who in some people's eyes are ideal employees because busy-ness is their "fix." Yet, inevitably, they work themselves into illness or death without being any more productive than the smart workers around them who have plenty of energy and time left over from work to live full and balanced lives.

Comments and Reflections: How is it in your organizational culture—is it okay to just sit and reflect or read an article or book in your field? How is it in your personal life? Must you always be busy at something—some project or activity? Do you take time to think things through before starting something, or do you throw yourself into it and then find that you have to do a lot of things over again because a mistake was made the first time that could have been avoided with a little thought? _____

_____

_____

_____

_____

_____

_____

_____

_____

_____

CHAPTER 23

Levels of Transformation

[Conversation over dinner]

Tom: I was walking around my place the other day. At last, spring is really here in southern Indiana and you know how explosive that is! I'm always amazed at the lavishness and power of life, especially evident in the spring. The experience started me thinking about transformations.

Alan: Say some more.

Tom: You know I will! When you think about it, everything is constantly transforming or changing from one state of being into another. Transforming simply means that the present form of something is undergoing a transition or change to a different form. An acorn planted in the earth transforms into an oak seedling, then a tree; a caterpillar transforms into a pupa, then into a butterfly or moth. "State of being" means the condition something is in at any one moment.

So you can say that work transforms states of being too. Different levels of an organization work on different but connected levels of transformation. Organizations that do their transforming best on all levels and in all areas tend to survive and flourish.

The most basic level is material transformation. I say "most basic" because it is the most visible and straightforward. It requires little or no waste of time, effort, delays, rework or scrap if done by skillful workers and machines whose processes are in control. Various tools, techniques, and methods can be employed to design and operate in a way that achieves continuous improvement of the material transforming process. In an automobile plant, for example, raw materials such as forgings and castings are transformed into more complex materials like component parts or finished products.

The second level is that which transforms data. Data are bits of information, knowledge, facts, needs, specifications. Useful data can be collected and systematized to create information. Useless data are classified as noise. The amount and pace of data transforming have increased enormously with the computer age. These amazing machines very quickly process data into reports, forecasts, spreadsheets, letters, invoices, graphs, and matrices—in short, into hundreds of different configurations managers increasingly feel they cannot do without.

Data transformation may also involve converting customer needs (data) into new products, product design changes, manufacturing changes, or service changes. It may also mean applying technological knowledge directly to material changes, as in computer-aided design and manufacturing, or—more recently—computer integrated manufacturing. It could also mean transforming human needs into compensation changes, benefits changes, or other personnel-related policy changes. This process is less visible than material transformation, but more powerful in that it guides and directs what occurs at the material level. A small bit of new knowledge can totally transform a material process. Replacing the transistor with the computer chip is a dramatic example.

A third, even more subtle transformation, is that which occurs in mental or emotional changes. All of us work from a mental and emotional state of being based on the frameworks within which we define our reality. When we adopted these frameworks, usually when we were children, they served very well to help us make sense of the world, and to survive in it. Even when these frameworks no longer serve us well and we wish to transform them, we may not be able to, because changing them requires us to understand how we think. This means understanding the way our values work (our real values, not necessarily the ones we say we hold), how we judge and compare, how we screen information in or out, how our biases and prejudices operate, how we create images to react to—in other words, how we're conditioned. These are the mechanisms that we use to create our mental frameworks. To transform our mental/emotional state we must construct new frameworks that allow us to operate differently. This reconstruction is even more powerful than data transformation, since a slight change in framework brings revolutionary changes in the ways we convert data into information. For example, when a person is made the director of a department and now sees herself as responsible for its success, as opposed to merely a contributor, many of the old data messages that she could once ignore suddenly become important sources of information.

These different levels of transformation are all important and interconnected. In the absence of consciousness at a higher level, the lower levels will tend to guide and direct all our thinking.

Alan: You mean that people operating from a material level of awareness can't get beyond material transformation issues, because they can't recognize and use data that apply to higher levels? Such an awareness level leaves us with a mental framework that is totally reactive to outside material events—what we commonly call "firefighting." A classic statement of this level of awareness would be, "If it ain't broke, don't fix it."

Tom: Right. Continuing with your example, operating from the data—rather than from the material—level is more powerful because it allows us to anticipate mechanical breakdowns and take preventive measures. In that way, instead of waiting for the machine to break down before we fix it, we can control the material level. But at this level the mental/emotional elements often remain unconscious, and opportunities for creative shifts will usually be missed. This is so because data are always processed through a mental framework that has certain habitually preferred options that are never questioned unless they fail.

Alan: Taking it the next step, then, to work from the mental/emotional level is to create visions of possibilities and become aware of new frameworks that open previously unseen doors. So, for example, on this level we might create a machine that never breaks down, or a process that avoids using machines altogether.

Tom: That's right. This level uses data and material in ways that go beyond those currently accepted and understood by "experts," who are called that because on the data level they have mastered the various options accepted as correct in their fields of expertise.

Working effectively on the mental/emotional level requires an awareness of our own mental processes and the mental processes of those we lead. With this understanding we can lead others to new transformative capabilities at the data and material levels.

These same thinking levels can be applied to our own persons. Our material is our body, our data are our knowledge, values, and sense perceptions, and our mental/emotional level is our thinking and feeling process—both conscious and intuitive. Through practice, becoming more aware of the connections helps us realize how these levels work organizationally.

Comments and Reflections

CHAPTER 24

Value
and Quality

[In a seminar on quality]

Tom: We pay attention to the present through our senses. However, at any given moment we may elect to disregard our sensory impressions and focus on some internal thought or idea or image. The temptation to tune into these internal matters is usually motivated by assigning them a higher value than whatever is informing our senses at the moment. Most of us seem to treat our personal mental agenda as more valuable than almost anything sensed in the present. What is this but self-centeredness? We all know people—perhaps ourselves—who only want to play out their own agendas and tune out everyone else's.

Alan: I know it has taken me years of practice to pay attention to what my eyes and ears are bringing to me, and I still have a hard time with the senses of smell, touch, and taste, unless the stimuli are really powerful. I brought along this letter from my file that describes what frequently happens in hierarchical organizations.

Dear Boss:

You keep encouraging me to come in and talk over any problems or issues that I haven't come across or that I need some help with. That's good. Whenever I've asked to talk to you about such matters, you have made time for me within a day or two at the most. That's good too. But typically when I come in and sit down, I say a couple of sentences, then you cut in—sometimes to disagree, sometimes to make a comment about what I've just said, sometimes to change the subject entirely. Once, I recall you started talking about an argument you had had with one of your kids the night before.

I can't remember a time when I left your office feeling that I had been given air time and had been heard, except once or twice when both of us had loose schedules. On those occasions I was finally able to get my issue across by inserting a sentence here and there when you had stopped to take a breath.

I feel like the bartender in the old cartoon who has grabbed the customer by the necktie and is saying, "Now let me tell you my problems!" As soon as you hear that I want to see you, I think you start planning how you're going to fill the available time just in case what I want to discuss will expose your ignorance or put you on the spot. The result is frustration for me. I'd rather you would put me off—except that I know you expect me to talk to you and I do respect your experience and ideas when you do share them with me off the cuff.

I don't expect you always to find time for me or always to agree with my perspective on things. But I do wish you'd show me enough respect to hear me out. As it is, I seldom sense that you've really understood my issue and I feel discounted by your inattention. That's not good for me, for you, for us, or for the company.

Given the fact that we are dealing with the relationship of quality to value, it seems that placing a high value on our own mental agenda, as the boss in this letter is apparently doing, can have a destructive effect on the quality, not only of his listening, but also of the relationship between him and his subordinate.

Tom: That's a good connection, and thanks for bringing the letter. Quality has to do with whether what we are doing is done with total attention to our sense perceptions. Doing something with quality is only possible when we are fully present at the time we do it. Watching and learning while doing can let us kaizen what we are watching, hearing, feeling (in the sense of touching), smelling, and tasting.

Alan: Tasting?

Tom: Sure. Good cooks are constantly tasting what they are doing so as to improve the flavor. If we are not present with all our senses, we will likely fail to notice those things that will allow us to improve the next time.

Now the value question steps back from the immediacy of the senses and asks, "should I be doing this at all? Does this specific activity add value to the overall connected process I am part of?" The boss in the letter seems to have concluded that it's valuable to have his subordinates come in to talk with him, but that the added value is primarily to have them listen to him, to link them into his process rather than seeing that both are involved in some larger process that only his senses can reveal. Obviously if we cannot see the overall process of which we are all a part, then the question of how we add value is unanswerable.

Alan: The value-added question becomes tricky when it's applied to work that does not produce tangible, material products that show us the improvements we make right as we make them. What is value added in managing and developing people? What is value added in information sharing?

Tom: As we have seen in the letter, it is in these realms that ego-driven agendas often take precedence. The problem is that by shutting down our attention to our sense perceptions we may never grasp the connections. Here's the dilemma: we don't know the value connection, so we don't pay attention; we can't learn the value connection, because we aren't paying attention. We get stuck in meetings and efforts that keep us baffled.

Quality is doing things right, or correctly; value is doing the right things, those things that add value. The two go together. Some "results only" people think only value is important, but if we do the right things poorly no one wants the low-quality result. Combining the two is necessary for quality performance. In the short term we can push for performance only, but if we are unaware of how things work and are not paying attention to what is going on, improvements will not be possible, and serious harm may even result.

For example, we might remove the air filter on our automobile, having heard that the car is more powerful without it. For a short time we enjoy the extra power as a result of more oxygen getting to the combustion chamber. And because we do not understand the need for clean air in the system, we congratulate ourselves for getting such good results, and even begin to believe we are better engineers than those who designed the engine. Eventually, however, the dirty air will clog the fuel and combustion systems, leading to a costly breakdown in the quality of engine performance.

Most cost-cutting efforts are aimed at eliminating non-value-added work. Such efforts are commendable to the degree that the work eliminated truly does not add value. But very seldom does someone's work add no value at all. Value added and waste are all mixed in together the way fat is marbleized in a choice steak. Therefore chaos often ensues when workers are eliminated, because others are neither aware of how their work interconnects with other work in the organization, nor of the specific actions that make up the value-added portions. That is why it is better to reduce costs by having those who perform the work identify and eliminate the waste by increasing their awareness and attention.

When separated or set in opposition, value and quality cannot be achieved. On the personal level, when we watch ourselves in action, we will notice recurring patterns of behavior that, with minor changes, may both add value and contribute higher quality to our lives. Staying in the present, with all our senses alert until the connection is made, will help us act purposefully.

Comments and Reflections

CHAPTER 25

Quality, Process, and Results Thinking

[More from the quality seminar]

Tom: Quality thinking is process thinking. Process control and quality control are interrelated and are essentially the same. Quality control done perfectly means that there is no waste in the many processes that come together to create a product or service for a customer.

When you think about it, there is nothing *but* process. Whether it is a machine process, assembly process, planning process, measuring process, interaction process, meeting process, or anything else involving action, process never ends. If that is true, then what about results? Results are simply snapshots of processes to see how the process is doing at one particular point. If we take this notion seriously, we see that results are illusions of fixity amidst the flow of process.

Alan: So why do we like to think results instead of process?

Tom: Well, there are some things we can say in favor of results thinking. It is superior to activity thinking, by which I mean the notion that to be busy doing something, whatever it is, is all there is to life and work. Requiring results at least forces all these activities to achieve something. Results thinking also provides us with goals or milestones we wish to achieve. If one is creating something, whether a machine or a work of art, he or she has an idea of what is desired before the work is begun. Without that conception, the work would have no direction; one bolt or weld would be as good as another, as would one color of paint or one brushstroke. Mere activity without form or direction is nothing but wasted energy.

But results thinking often gives us the sense that we are in control of what will happen. If we set objectives and goals and measure results, we often think we can control direction. This sense is illusory, especially so in organizations, but I believe it is why results thinking is so popular with so many managers. But these stated goals and objectives are seldom congruent with the processes currently at work that are supposed to create them. Results-oriented thinkers frequently state desired goals over and over again in the frustrated hope that *this* time they will be successful when the process that fails to deliver remains the same.

Alan: I've heard that one definition of insanity is believing results can be changed without changing the processes that create them.

Tom: Quality thinking requires us to see the movement of processes in both time and space. All processes evolve with time. This evolutionary change can be seen in terms of growth, trends, flows, assembly lines, learning curves, and other measures of movement.

Since any process will change over time the trick is to be directing the change, adding value along the way. If we cannot see and think in process terms, we cannot direct it and add value. Quality thinking requires the ability to focus on a process over a time span, seeing both what is happening in the present and what kinds of changes are occurring in what direction.

Processes are interconnected and functioning together at any one moment in a given space. No process stands alone. The world and work consist of a complex web of processes pushing and pulling in various directions. If we can see the dynamics of this multitude of interactions, then we can direct them to serve some common purpose, like serving a customer or building an engine. Quality thinking requires this perception of dynamic connections between processes. Not to see them blinds us to the sources of many problems which, if not corrected, will keep us continually in a reactive mode.

Quality thinking as process awareness is key to eliminating waste. Processes are ongoing, everywhere interconnected and always changing. We can go with them, guiding and adjusting, or pretend that simply by demanding them we can get the desired performance and results with no understanding of how things work. This latter way is the road to confusion, frustration, and, as you have pointed out, even to madness—although more frequently it leads to resignation and a sense of powerlessness to do more than react to the next crisis.

We are not speaking here of a philosophy or a body of theory deduced from a set of theorems and held together by internal logical rules. Process thinking and process control are real time, subject to continual present observation and modification. In contrast, results thinking and results control are concerned with past time and future projection. Results control requires judgments about how things should be; process thinking is concerned with how things actually work. Process thinking is holistic; results thinking is fragmented. Process thinking looks for continuous improvements; results thinking looks for magical or miraculous shifts in outcomes.

Alan: Are you saying that results thinking is bad and wrong?

Tom: No more than we would say that looking at a photo of someone is wrong and that instead one should look only at the real person. If any wrongness is involved, it is in treating the photo as if it were the person himself or herself. The photo is static, locked in the past; the person is alive and changing. Photos are useful as reminders or as works of art. They can capture the fact that change has taken place through comparing pictures of the same person or object taken at different times, but they are not the change process itself.

Alan: So the difference between results thinking and process thinking is analogous to the difference between a snapshot and a movie, in which change is constantly occurring. The same can be said about financial statements of a business's condition: they are, as it were, "snapshots" of some moment in the business's past. In our desire to freeze things, to get a "fix" on them, we have often created a world of abstractions that block us from seeing the processes of life and change.

Exercise: In order to get some sense of process with respect to yourself, think of yourself as an evolving system. You are a living process in time and space with multiple subprocesses pushing and pulling you at every moment. To eliminate wasted effort in your life, you must begin by seeing these processes.

Reflect on the details of your daily life routine. What are some habits or practices that stand out as a "waste of time," or as serving no useful purpose? For example, how often do you move from your desk to some other location, when one trip would be sufficient? How often have you read a report containing lots of numbers and graphs purporting to tell you what's actually going on, when you are only a stone's throw from the activities being reported on? How many meetings do you call or attend, simply because you have always had them, or have always attended them, but nothing happened as a result? How many memos or reports have you read that made no difference in your life and work? How often do you call someone on the phone, hang up, and then call back again because you forgot something else you wanted to say? Why do you follow these practices? What positive things would happen if you stopped doing them? What negative things? What payoff do you get from continuing to do them? How could you change your processes to ones with less waste, and still get the payoff you need?

CHAPTER 26

Self-Reliance

Alan: In our fragmented, crisis-driven world, we are confronted with an interesting paradox. On one hand we believe strongly that self-reliance is good and important. On the other hand, we need more consultants, therapists, and other outside support than ever before. How do we reconcile this apparent contradiction?

Tom: An answer may be found in how self-reliance plays out in crisis-driven thinking. Most crisis-driven managers I have dealt with have a narrow idea of what it means to be self-reliant. For them, self-reliance means being in control of, on top of, ahead of, or possessing more power than those around them. Self-reliance means never having to ask for support, or better yet, never needing or understanding how to use the support systems and processes that surround them in everyday life. They want to be heroes who do it alone, without any help from anybody or anything.

Alan: Who is the truly self-reliant person as you think about her or him?

Tom: I believe it is one who is in tune with her or his supporting environment and depends on self to live in that environment harmoniously and productively. There are no self-reliant people—self-reliant in this sense—who do not appreciate the many facets of the whole system they find themselves in. They work within and with that system for the benefit of both. As a negative example, most teenagers are not self-reliant, because they have no idea how or what it costs to operate a household. They live in the illusion of self-reliance because they never have to ask, let alone answer, questions about rent, food, utilities, gasoline, furniture, plumbers, tools, insurance, interest, and the myriad hidden but necessary domestic expenses and requirements.

I once spoke with a high school class about basic financial management. They believed they could have a good life and raise children on today's equivalent of $500 a month. They thought they were grown-up and self-reliant, but did not comprehend or understand the environment they would be in. Not to know your environment well gives the lie to self-reliance.

Alan: I'm reminded of all the articles in major business magazines that make it sound like the CEO has worked all the miracles of change in his or her organization, without any help from anyone else. That myth of the self-made, heroic individual is certainly pervasive in our culture.

Tom: It certainly is. Self-reliance does sound to us like rugged American individualism or the self-made "man," but it is really a quality of wholeness in the world. Self-reliance does not mean not needing others, but refers to knowing how to rely on one's true self in a system of others. It does not deny the necessity of support, but stresses learning and using the natural support existing within any environment. Self-reliance can't be developed without understanding and being sensitive to the surrounding environment.

Alan: And I assume that when you speak of environment, you not only mean the environment of the organization, but of the business and larger world environment as well. Then there is also the internal environment of the individual, by which I mean the mental and emotional capabilities that one brings to the work.

Tom: That's a good point. We are all aware of individuals who support others, not in an interdependent sense but out of a sense of inadequacy. They are quick to see the need for support and provide it very well, but feel personally powerless when left on their own. They seem to be able to do only for others. (Although this trait is traditionally ascribed to women, it is by no means limited to one gender.) Self-reliant people play supporting roles to develop positive and productive work environments, while at the same time they become increasingly self-reliant in their ability to become personally empowered in the overall system.

Alan: In other words, as they support others, they study the system to see how their roles can work within the system to add value. In that way they come to understand the system better and learn to be more effective workers in it.

Tom: Yes. This is what I call being whole in the system. You know, I have been accused of not modeling the positive use of support because I seldom ask for it from my colleagues. But I do constantly get support through a self-reliant method of working. I am always using the workplace environment to give and receive support. I rely on myself to learn from that, because only I can learn for myself. At the same time I also see that I do nothing alone in this environment, so I am always exchanging with others. I give, they receive, and vice versa.

Here we get into kaizen thinking. To understand what you are a part of requires that you learn about operations and designs of your environment. I am amazed at managers who know minute quantitative details of outcomes and results (sales, profits, costs, people, customers, suppliers, parts, shortages, etc.), and yet know so little about how everything operates or how it is designed. These managers see themselves as self-reliant and strong, but when it comes to changing the system or operation, they call on consultants because they have no clue as to where or how to begin. An organization comprised of managers like these is out of control.

Alan: Summarizing, to be self-reliant is to be whole in the world. To be whole is to appreciate oneself and to be interdependent with the environment and with others. To appreciate the environment, others, and become self-reliant, together we must learn continuously.

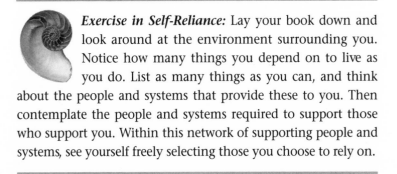

Exercise in Self-Reliance: Lay your book down and look around at the environment surrounding you. Notice how many things you depend on to live as you do. List as many things as you can, and think about the people and systems that provide these to you. Then contemplate the people and systems required to support those who support you. Within this network of supporting people and systems, see yourself freely selecting those you choose to rely on.

CHAPTER 27

Courage and the Change to Quality

[Still more from the quality seminar]

Tom: Courage is probably the most significant attribute needed in our culture to change to a high-quality kaizen-focused organization. It takes courage to have, and keep unflinchingly, a clarity of vision and purpose that consistently guides actions amidst the demands and crises abounding in any system. I have found that most leaders are trying to satisfy or please someone else and have no inner sense of purpose. This is to be expected in a culture like ours that identifies quarterbacks or high academic achievers as leaders: people who have been most successful in pleasing the coach or the teacher.

I learned about courage and leadership as president of my college fraternity. Our house was physically falling apart as a result of too many toga parties; we had a shrinking membership and were nearly bankrupt. I hadn't realized how bad things had become until I assumed office. I decided that our long-term survival depended on getting the total house in order. I called a halt to drinking parties in the house, forced members to pay late dues or lose privileges, fined participants in food fights, and stopped destructive pledge harassment. As if those prohibitions weren't enough, I initiated clean-up processes and dreamed up constructive projects for pledges.

The upshot of all this massive change was outright revolt by the majority of the membership. They constantly threatened me with impeachment at house meetings, with physical harm when they rolled home drunk on Saturday nights, and even my friends shunned me or gave me the silent treatment. A few supporters stood behind me—usually far behind.

Being alone during that turnaround period showed me the price one has to pay to change a culture. I had to be consistent even with those few supporters who thought they could get away with a minor infraction, like having a beer in the house, because they were my friends. At one point or another, everyone in the house was angry at me.

By the end of my term of office the house was in good repair, we were financially solvent, and the membership had doubled. The members, once so angry, had begun to develop pride in the house, and almost everyone came to me and apologized.

What I learned from this experience was that leading a cultural change is a day-to-day personal process requiring persistence and the courage to stand against the accustomed ways. The feelings that resulted from being ostracized, ignored, criticized, threatened, and otherwise assaulted challenged my vision and purpose. It would have been easy for me to strike back and attack my attackers, or just give in. Instead I simply held to my purpose and vision, dealing with issues as they arose, as much as possible in ways that advanced the vision I held for how the house could be. I was alternately active and passive, taking initiative when I could and letting events happen when I could do nothing, confident that certain helping forces were in play.

To this day I don't know why I risked my friendships and acceptance to turn a fraternity operation around. It certainly was not going to make a great deal of difference in the world. It just became clear to me that wasting all those physical and human resources was simply wrong, and that I was in a position to do something about it. Before being elected president I would hardly have been described as a courageous leader. As a matter of fact, I was a good example of the opposite: an uninspired follower. Something inside me erased that old "tape" that told me to play it safe and just go along. At this comparatively young age I realized that I could trust what I saw as possible and act purposefully to create it.

It is only in hindsight that I see myself as acting courageously in this situation. At the time I did what needed to be done with outward calm. Inwardly I felt scared and alone, yet I was also inspired by what I saw coming into being.

Alan: Unfortunately, courage today is often seen as betting the company on high-risk decisions, massively reducing personnel, ordering people around, threatening or intimidating the forces arrayed against change. Seldom does one see a person inspired by a vision that enrolls herself or himself and others and permits the quiet courage of commitment to take root.

In two companies where I worked, those of us who created a vision wanted others to support it immediately as testimony to its rightness. When easy agreement and enthusiastic support were not forthcoming, most of us visionaries abandoned the effort. We needed others' approval to provide the energy to persevere. Only later did I realize that acceptance and support do not come easily, even among the visionary group members, assuming there is more than one. As your account indicates, the person or persons holding the vision may have to persevere—often against great resistance—for a long time before others begin to make that vision their own and invest their own positive energies into realizing it.

Tom: Even without a vision of some desirable condition we want to create, we may carry out courageous acts of firefighting or problem solving. We come to think that courage is to be first, fastest, brightest, and strongest in doing what everyone already wants done—like leading the troops to victory. That does require courage of a kind, but not the kind we are describing. This kind of courage is that which from the outset empowers us to act virtually alone if we must, pulled toward the future by a compelling mental picture of something better that could be, though it is outside the accepted norm and no one as yet knows how to do it—like the invention by the founding fathers of the United States of America.

Our need for change today requires the courage of a James Madison or an Einstein, or others who did not live in accordance with the culture's accepted norms. Usually most of us at first will dismiss such people as crazy dreamers. We will continue to live and think in the ways that are comfortable, maintaining the status quo and resisting change. Eventually, however, the courageous leader who persists in following his or her vision will be vindicated, and a new way will become the obvious one to pursue.

Alan: I suppose that in any discussion of visionary leadership someone like Adolph Hitler inevitably comes to mind. Like it or not, he clearly fits the criteria of visionary leadership. I think we cannot ignore the fact that not all visions are beneficial. Some may envision and create evil consequences.

Tom: That's true, especially within the framework of massive political entities, like nation-states, that derive their existence from mythic thinking, although we can see the same kind of thing even in small groups. In business organizations, however, which are surrounded by actual competitors and are dependent for their existence on actual customers and suppliers and especially actual employees, visions must be seen as worthy and beneficial to all those who have some stake in their survival and health. For that reason it's hard for me to imagine a corporate "Hitler" creating a destructive vision and winning massive followership.

Alan: I have been involved in a couple of situations where the top management group created a vision for the organization, but the plant manager and CEO almost immediately resumed practices that were opposed to what we said we wanted to create. When I would talk to other managers about the vision and the power of visioning, most would dismiss the whole process by saying that when they saw the top person doing what the vision called for, then they might take it seriously, but not before. I found it very difficult to persevere in bringing the vision to reality without support from the top. Unfortunately, I got into judging and blaming the top person in both cases, rather than simply focusing on my own efforts in the departments I could affect.

Tom: It does make things much more difficult when there is little or no support from the top. And of course the situation can be made impossible when judgmentalism and blaming enter the picture, as you found out. But it is possible to make significant headway even in difficult circumstances, especially if data can be collected showing that what you're doing in your own area is having significant positive results of a kind the manager or CEO recognizes and respects.

Exercise in Acting Courageously: Reflect on a time when you stood alone on an issue. How did you feel? Were you fearful and or angry toward those who opposed you? How did you resolve the tension you felt? If you have never stood alone for something in which you believed strongly, think of something at work that you believe is non-productive or destructive, but no one will raise it as an issue. What does it feel like to consider breaking the silence of the group? How might you take action in a way that is not blaming or harmful to others, yet maintains your conviction and clarity on the issue?

CHAPTER 28

Continuous Improvement and Quality

[from the seminar on quality]

Tom: Kaizen of everything we do is crucial for prolonged success in business, personal life, and society. In business and industry most of us have depended on major innovations and technological breakthroughs for our quality gains. These breakthroughs are important, but in those periods between major new capital investments lie many opportunities for everyone to contribute to improvements in the ways things are currently done. "Quantum-jumping innovations" usually come with big price tags or major production and systems realignments, and typically come from highly educated technical experts. We Americans have come to believe that these big, sweeping changes are the only way to go, but significant improvement can also be made gradually through continually adjusting, refining, and upgrading by people who actually perform the work, aided and supported by technicians and engineers. Then, when a great innovation comes along, everyone will know the system well and fit that innovation easily into the operation.

Alan: Unfortunately, continuous improvement, as you have just described it, is atypical. For most working people in this country there is only maintenance of the status quo. They are told to keep the machine going, keep up with the schedule, handle the emergencies. Everyone hopes someone will come up with the "great idea" that will solve the mess. It seems that, whether in politics or business, we all wish for a hero who will deliver us from our difficulties. Why are we so obsessed with major breakthroughs and great ideas? Why do we miss the day-to-day opportunities to improve?

Tom: Our approach to quality process control in this country gives some insights into possible answers to these questions. Historically we have measured quality as either "in spec" or out. The part passed or it did not. The machine ran or it didn't. Everything is either/or in this world of thinking. We made it nice and neat, black and white, on or off. Measures were used to determine good or bad, right or wrong. This tendency pervades our culture. We want things to be clearly right or wrong. We don't like gray. We want to have bad people to blame for what's wrong. In short, we don't like to be in touch with things as they really are.

Today, we are beginning to understand that quality is constant improvement toward some target of exactness. Trends are measured to see if movement is being made toward that target. Either/or thinking has no place in such a view. We have current capability and an improving trend. Just getting results within specifications is not acceptable over the long term.

Alan: If what you say is true, some significant change is required in the way we view the world. What's the shift we need to make to move us into this mode of continuous improvement?

Tom: First, we must acknowledge that we are usually up in our heads musing about yesterday or tomorrow. These are the minds that create innovations, that attack yesterday's problem and figure out a new solution for tomorrow. Such minds are appropriate for scientists or others whose job it is to find new solutions. But for the most part the rest of us just get down on ourselves, because we are not gifted with the ability to invent new solutions. But most of us have a real contribution to make. Our job is to be present in the here and now and to make continuous improvement, because it is only in the present that opportunities for improvement can be seen. Unfortunately most of us do not have our eyes and ears open to perceive what is actually happening because we believe that we have nothing to offer. When we do open them, we often find that we really do not know how anything works.

Alan: You pointed out earlier that continuous improvement requires non-judgmental investigation of how things are working right now. A Japanese consultant we know observed that American managers don't know how just to watch what's going on. We must be non-judgmental, because viewing things as right or wrong, good or bad, is destructive to the very act of observing. Our seeing and thinking close down when we judge.

Tom: Yes, that's one of the superordinate principles. We must also be non-judgmental toward ourselves. Suppose, when we open our eyes and ears to what is actually going on, we don't understand at first what we see. If we are judgmental of ourselves, we will stop paying attention to what is there and begin accusing ourselves of stupidity or some other fault. Judgments create reactive defenses or positions, rather than clarity of observation, which is what we're after. Quality process improvement requires straight and honest data about actual operation. There is no need for excuses, opinions, suppositions, defenses, positions, or interpretations, which serve only to cloud the simple actualities and therefore create waste.

Continuous improvement toward quality requires the continual elimination of waste. Therefore, we must begin to awaken and see what's in front of our eyes. At least for a short while we must forget all the theories, opinions, desires, regrets, and intentions that fill our heads with distracting noise.

When that noise is quieted, even momentarily, we are able to see what is actually going on. From this point of clarity we are enabled to see, comprehend, and, with practice, understand. Then we can discover opportunities for improvement.

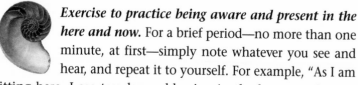

Exercise to practice being aware and present in the here and now. For a brief period—no more than one minute, at first—simply note whatever you see and hear, and repeat it to yourself. For example, "As I am sitting here, I see tree leaves blowing in the breeze, red roses, tawny fields laced with green, an old secretary desk, birds singing, a set of encyclopedias, the words forming on the monitor screen, the hum of the computer," etc. Make no judgments, simply observe and move on.

You may find this exercise fatiguing at first. If it is, shorten the time of doing it, but do it at regular intervals during the day. When you find yourself going into your head (thinking about something removed in time or space) or making some judgment about something you see or hear, be aware of that as well, and move on.

CHAPTER 29

Energy and Process Control

Tom: One cannot talk about process without talking about energy. Energy is the basis of everything that exists. That is essentially what E=MC means. In advanced industrial economies the energy available to us for production of goods and services incurs monetary cost of some kind. Whether it is human energy in the form of wages, machine energy in the form of capital equipment, or fuel energy in the forms of electricity, gas, or petroleum, the common element is that energy expended incurs cost. In this sense time is also energy since, whenever the other forms of energy are available but not being used, potential energy is lost. If we think of money as a form of energy, this aspect of time is very clear. Money can be used to "work" and make more money. If time is lost in putting the money to work, then energy is lost. In this concept, energy takes many forms, from fairly gross and material energy, like parts of a machine, to highly abstract energy like time. But in all cases, the chief concern of those who are in the business of providing goods and services is that of using energy in all its forms as efficiently as possible, i.e., at the least cost, to satisfy customer needs.

Alan: If I follow your line of thinking, you are saying that the purpose of all organizing processes is to transform energy into another, more desired form at the least cost. In a market economy we understand cost purely in monetary terms, but in nature it refers to preservation of the environment and all constituent elements of it: air and water quality; animal and plant species; soils, etc.

Tom: That's right. By all organizing processes we mean plants, animals, people, businesses, nations—in short, anything natural or human that brings constituent elements together to serve some purpose.

For our thinking here, we will concentrate on business organizations and people—the processes with which we are most familiar. In machining operations, energy transforms material from rough to finished states through various refining or other value-adding processes. Machining a part to a certain size is the application of machine energy to the coarser energy form of a part. The more energy of all kinds required to achieve the desired size and shape, the more value—and therefore cost—is added to the finished part.

But as you can see in this example, energy is neither created nor destroyed. It is only transformed. At certain points energy can take transformative "leaps." An example of one of these leaps may be found in the man-machine relationship. A person may be doing a job manually, using all his or her mental and physical energy to do the task. Then this person invents a machine or tool that cuts the human energy expenditure in half. He or she now has 50% more available energy. Human energy has essentially been transformed into machine energy, because the machine is now doing the work a human being was once required to perform. The more creative human mental energy is available to invent other transformations. Another transformational leap occurs within us when we take in nourishment. In the digestive system, food energy changes into higher level human mental energy in ways still not fully understood.

This transformation of energy occurs by means of processes. At the lower end of unrefined energy/matter, the transforming process is easily seen and managed. Ore heated under the right conditions changes into iron. As we move to higher levels of complexity, it becomes more difficult to see and manage the transforming process.

In business organizations, managers have tended to overlook process and focus on results. But to focus on the result is to look at only one point of transformation to see if the desired level of refinement has been obtained. However, energy (and cost) has already been expended, and if what has been obtained is not what is desired, then even more energy is required to correct it. In some cases the result of the entire process must be scrapped. In both instances waste and consequent cost are incurred. Thus, focusing only on results can be costly and ineffective. Most serious is that a results-only focus leads us to believe that we do not have to learn and understand the transforming process as a whole. Once that understanding is lost, both the process and its supporting systems are out of control, and when errors occur we do not know how to begin correcting them.

Managing and controlling a process of energy transformation require that we understand the process and that we have clear and accurate data about its real-time functioning; in other words, about what it is actually doing at any given moment. With respect to a machine work station, understanding includes the machine operating process itself and its underlying support systems. In a business, managers must understand the entire production system, from supplier to end user or customer. Long-term viability is ensured by enhancing the overall system's capability to transform at ever-higher levels of efficiency and at ever-lower levels of waste—and it is management's job to see that that happens.

Alan: I'm thinking about this topic applied to human physiology. In our metabolic process, our bodies automatically transform food into higher physical and mental energy. We do not need to understand the process consciously for it to work, luckily for us. But being able to use that source of physical and mental energy more effectively requires a more conscious transformation. Through practice on the physical and mental levels, we learn movements and manual skills. When it comes to purely mental processes, the task of understanding and mastery becomes more difficult.

Tom: Yes, it is possible to use our mental energy to transform ideas into action or states of being. The difficulty is that we try to manage the results without understanding the system or how to gather clear data. For example, some event may result in our feeling strong negative emotions. These may lead to interpersonal conflict, confusion, inability to act, fear, anxiety, frustration, and other stressful behaviors and attendant feelings. All these actions and emotions require energy, but this energy is almost always expended wastefully with great psychic cost.

Studying the self as a system and learning how to get clear data on ourselves is the best way to improve personal effectiveness. The similarity between ourselves and other transforming systems can give us insights into improving all levels of work, and it can also illuminate how we ourselves function. These connections do not appear on the surface but at the deeper level of energy transformations. Thinking about whatever we work on and know well in these terms will help us improve our own personal and professional effectiveness.

Exercise in separating certain words from the negative energy they generate: Reflect on a recent occasion when you experienced some strong negative emotion at work, whether fear, anxiety, anger or something else. (Preferably, focus on an event in which you felt an emotion you most commonly feel.) See yourself in that situation, picture it clearly: place, people present, the issues being discussed, etc. What was it that "pushed your button"? A person's remark, some interruption, a misprint in a report, a gesture, whatever. At what or at whom was your emotion directed? Now think about what the remark or action symbolized for you (threat, stupidity, ignorance, insult, accusation, etc.). How do you connect those words with the emotion you felt? (Remember, words are only words; they signify nothing in and of themselves—only what meanings we assign to them.) Think back to the occasions in your early life when you set these "button-pushing" words or actions into their negative context. Who were the people in this original context? What was the situation? Is it the same situation as the recent one you have just experienced?

Now think about the words or actions that evoked your response. Think about them one at a time, out of context. Do they contain any inherent emotional content? Say them over to yourself several times aloud, and each time say, "just a word," or "just an action."

CHAPTER 30

Controlling
Process vs Outcomes

[Another "war story" from Tom]

Tom: When I was a finance clerk in the army, I learned a valuable lesson on the difference between process and outcome. One of the many generals who passed through our division made a big push for selling savings bonds to the troops. At the time, USO shows and ads in *Stars and Stripes* were stressing the idea that U.S. Savings Bonds were a good investment. The general knew who was behind all the ballyhoo. The Pentagon, he was sure, would smile on his efforts—especially if they were successful.

He issued a proclamation that our division would spearhead the drive with at least 90% participation. As a good leader, the general promoted the goal over and over as being good for the troops. As for us troops, who were rather poorly paid, this proudly hailed outcome only sounded like having less money available to spend on our modest pleasures.

After the first month of the campaign, we payroll clerks reported that participation was 45%. This news outraged the general. (Heavens, how would he look to his Pentagon superiors!) He decided to have the payroll clerks spend time counseling—read persuading—the troops to buy bonds. His decision meant extra work for us, so we got together and decided to change the numbers. (Accountants are the only people in the world who can change results.) The next month we reported 94% participation and the general, who never bothered to check the numbers, was able to brag about his division. This amazing percentage of participation even made the papers.

The general believed he had led the troops to achieve his desired outcome. Aside from any questionable ethical practices, this episode showed me the fallacy of concentrating only on outcomes with the illusion that one can control them. An outcome or result is only as good as the process that creates it.

Controlling outcomes is what most of us strive to do most of the time. The number of desired outcomes a normal person tries to control is enormous.

Alan: How do you mean?

Tom: Well, when you think about it, every desire we have has a fantasized outcome attached to it, as does every fear. Each aspect of ourselves has multiple desires totally disconnected from the other aspects. We are somewhat like a large factory where each department and each function and each individual have separate, and often conflicting, desires with attached outcomes.

Within ourselves, we too confront multiple conflicting desires as they arise. Today I want a big dessert, tomorrow I want to lose weight. Constant confusion reigns. Hidden behind all these desires is our process of being. How do we function to create all these conflicting desires and their fantasized outcomes? What is our process? Can we look inside to find insights?

So long as we try to control outcomes only, we are helpless to do anything. We can curse and scream and demand and cry, but emotional outbursts don't enable us to understand how our process works so that we may integrate and improve it.

Most of us can't do what we desire because we don't know how we work. We can choose to act differently, and thus achieve desired outcomes, only if we know how we work. Otherwise we are only wishing to act in some different way and hoping it will magically happen. In this way, we're trapped by thinking only of outcomes.

At a simple level, outcomes as tools for gauging a moment in process are useful. For instance, the preparation and cooking process transforms raw food into an outcome, dinner. But if we don't eat the outcome right away (and don't refrigerate), the process continues and two days later we have a different outcome—garbage! What was dinner becomes something very different, because the process continues. Only at a specific moment is it a dinner. If we eat the dinner at the appropriate time, another, slightly different process commences.

Alan: Let me digest that for a moment. So, as we develop our being to become more capable of achieving outcomes, we take a momentary definition to mark progress along the way. But that definition is not the same as a title or position conferred upon us by someone else. For example, the general in your account received his title from the army and, believing it about himself, defined himself as a person in command of others. Therefore, he thought all he had to do was command an outcome and it would happen. He didn't take time to understand how the total process—including himself—worked so that when a certain command was given, the forces in play would create a process that would deliver the desired results.

Tom: That's true. He hadn't a notion what motivated the troops or us clerks in the office. To control the process of anything is to go deeply into its workings. Such probing can be extremely difficult and time-consuming. It is best to begin by just seeing and comprehending the process without attempting to control it. After much study, we can possibly see enough to intervene. The problem is that most of us desire results immediately, so we try to control ourselves or others before we really comprehend how we work. Again, the definitions we apply to ourselves blind us to our real being. We say we want to accomplish something—in the general's case, getting the bonds sold; then parts of us do something to give us the illusion of getting it done—issuing the command—and we are satisfied for a while, believing the falsified figures. Sooner or later, however, the truth comes out that nothing has been accomplished, but by that time we've gone on to something else.

Alan: I know that, with respect to old unwanted behavior habits, just when I think I'm over them they come back.

Tom: When we are beginning the process of self-understanding, it is difficult simply to be with the process when it shows us self-definitions we don't like—for example, that we are arrogant or conceited or deceitful. After being with them for awhile, we begin to see behind the definitions into how we actually work—our process, not our result. Eventually we begin to see that we have no hard and fast definitions; we are simply in the process of being, and in that process we sometimes act arrogantly, sometimes deceitfully, but also sometimes humbly and honestly. We may add up net worth, or show possessions or accomplishments, but they are the trappings of our being and not essential to it. It is our misfortune when we mistake the trappings for the essence.

Alan: Similarly, statistics are used to control machine processes, because quality cannot be controlled without a device to observe how well the machine is performing over time. This statistical history builds the base of observation. Once a deviation is noticed, the machine can be adjusted. Of course, the adjustment must be made by one who understands the machine and the impact of the adjustment. Someone without understanding would probably only make matters worse, despite best intentions. Once the process is in control, the outcomes only have to be monitored occasionally, since a process in control always assures the desired outcome.

Tom: And, that really is the way it is with ourselves. When we understand how we work, the outcomes will simply be noted. Understanding oneself is different from saying "I am this" or "I am that"—these are momentary definitions. It's different from listing our likes and dislikes. It's different from clarifying our values and beliefs. And it's not naming our problems or concerns. We are an interactive process with many different aspects struggling for control.

Finding our authentic essential being is not simple or easy. When we buy a package of breakfast food we are concerned with the contents, not with the packaging. Can we afford to be less concerned with our own being— our contents? Our packaging is our professed values, ideas, definitions, roles, self-images, desires, likes, dislikes, beliefs, prejudices, titles, accomplishments. To study the package is to miss the essence, and when we miss the essence, we miss everything.

Exercise to explore or discover one's essence: Have a trusted friend or spouse ask you this question: "Who are you?" Then respond to it with the first answer that comes to mind—your name, occupation, marital status, nationality, whatever. Then have your questioner ask, "Yes, and what else are you?" Continue this questioning and answering for as long as you can think of anything to say in the way of a description or definition. Pay attention to each answer you give and ask yourself, does this really capture my essence or is it a trapping? Eventually you may become aware that the answerer is different from the answers. Who is the answerer?

Another approach to discovering your core being is to meditate on this variation of a Zen *koan* (a paradox or riddle that cannot be answered by the rational thought process): Who were you before your father and mother were born?

CHAPTER 31

Fix vs Understand

Tom: We may face a dilemma in our workplaces: we feel the need for Kaizen thinking and irreversible improvement, but the approaches we take seem necessarily dictated by crises, and are therefore doomed to be short-term "patches" that don't last. Similarly, in our personal lives we consume great amounts of energy patching our floundering personal systems just to gain a short period of peace and quiet around the house. In both situations, new crises continually arise to increase our frustrations even more. The old patches either no longer work or work for shorter periods. We are caught in the vain exercise of trying to fix something we don't understand. Operational problems grow faster than we can investigate thoroughly. To someone consumed with the immediate need to "fix" something, advocating understanding the root causes of problems and then taking actions to eliminate them is usually met with the protest, "I just don't have time!"

Alan: I once worked in a transportation company where the greatest perennial problem was driver turnover. My boss was in such a panic about hiring drivers, he would approve almost any new scheme that he thought might bring new drivers into the company, no matter how much it cost or how damaging the long-term consequences might be. Several of us pointed out to him that the key was to retain as many as possible of the drivers we had, not to put all our effort into hiring from the dwindling supply. His response was that we did not know how to retain them, that the crisis was here and now, and that therefore we just had to concentrate all our efforts on hiring.

Tom: One of the basic issues is that we see "fixing" and "understanding" as separate pieces of work. We need to learn how to use fixes as a means to gain new and increased understanding.

Alan: But, as you've suggested, sometimes the "fixes" only obscure what's really going on, and so prevent us from moving toward a solid understanding.

Tom: That's right. Instead of continuing automatically to do what we have always done, we need to learn how to become truly experimental when we confront problems or new situations. Every system we have ever been part of—whether new or just new to us—has always had its share of problems to be fixed. If we had permission or freedom to do so, we experimented and began to notice how things within the system fit together and why things were done one way rather than another.

As a financial analyst, I found that most of my peers neither understood the overall intent of the financial control process, nor the way it was designed. By working on fixes and having a boss willing to answer questions, I redesigned my work and took a full-time job to half time. That allowed me to get involved with early attempts at office automation and management information systems. For me, the key is both fixing and learning systems at the same time. To fix something without knowing how and why it broke in the first place is setting yourself up to do it again later.

Alan: What I'm getting out of this conversation is that most people think of fixes as actions taken that are appropriate only to the breakage, whereas understanding requires thorough comprehension of the system, and actions appropriate to the comprehension.

Tom: Yes. In our personal lives it is the same. Most of us want to go off to some remote place to hide or escape from day-to-day problems while we spend time learning to "understand ourselves." Occasionally that is helpful, but limiting efforts at personal understanding to those "retreats" ensures a long learning curve, primarily because it removes us from the stage of actual practice into an artificial environment, and therefore the comprehension you speak of is lacking. The everyday fixes we make on ourselves open a window on who we are in our true context—which we have also helped to create. Then, rather than seeing our problems and frustrations only as pains to be avoided, we can see them as clues to opportunities for improvement through increased understanding.

The process might work this way. Let's say we have a negative encounter with a boss that causes us acute discomfort. For our own well being and job security we believe we have to "fix" the relationship. To us, fixing it usually means acting differently in order to placate or mollify our boss. More rarely, it means convincing the boss that she or he is wrong, thus justifying ourselves. As we work on either one of those courses of action, we disregard our own process, focusing instead on fixing something outside ourselves according to our own scenario. If we are successful we go on to other things; if not, we continue our attempts—always focused on the boss's response.

Alternatively, we can also focus on how we internally got into this situation in the first place. In the case cited above, disagreeing with someone in a position of power over us, where we end up scared and frustrated or self-justifying, is the way our "self" as a system has worked. In a situation like this, most of us would rather placate or focus on the issue and justify the rightness of our position than understand how our system works and how we got ourselves into the wrangle in the first place. We would rather be concilia-tors, or right, than effective.

If we were traveling by air to the West Coast and, as we were about to board the plane, an engine failed to start, we would expect a delay while the engine was repaired. If some-one in the next seat said, " I must get to L.A. I want to take off now," we would laugh at such immaturity and foolhardiness, because we would know that taking off with a bad engine is a recipe for disaster. But most of us do this every day when we demand certain outcomes without ever paying attention to our own operating process, system design, and underlying concepts. Somehow we think that we can get what we want out of a system, whether our own or that of our business, without investigating how and why it works as it does, and from that understanding, changing it so it will work better.

Alan: In any mechanical system, the true test of its ability is in its operation under normal working conditions. It is in actual application where fixes can lead to real insight about needed operations or design changes, but only when we use them to comprehend the system we're working with. To experiment in the laboratory or at the drawing board is appropriate at times, but the product or system must be employed, observed, and learned from as internal or end-user customers use it. True understanding, whether of prod-ucts or of ourselves, only comes from a combination of comprehension—a clear mental grasp of something—and action, that is, testing the comprehension by experimenting with various options and then practicing the chosen best option until capability is achieved.

For example, we all know that we cannot understand how to drive a car simply by studying a manual on how cars work—although a manual can be very helpful in our comprehension. We must actually get behind the wheel and begin driving the car. As we gain proficiency through practice, we may begin to experiment with it by taking cor-ners at various speeds, seeing how fast it can accelerate from a stop, how fast it can be brought to a standstill from various speeds. In that way, if we survive, we come to understand how to operate the car.

Tom: But frequently when we encounter problems with ourselves, many of us think that simply reading "the manual" will provide us with the understanding we need. How we deal with problems in our everyday lives provides us with the true book in whose pages we can gain insight and comprehension of how our personal systems operate. If they are dysfunctional, causing us unnecessary pain or even more complicated problems, we can change those systems to help us live lives of continuous growth and improvement. The opportunity to learn is always there before us in real-time events. It is not at some distant isolated retreat, in a book of "pop" psychology, or at the feet of some guru on a mountain top in Nepal. And the information we need is available within all of us, ready to instruct us whenever we wish.

Comments and Reflections _____

_____
_____
_____
_____
_____
_____
_____
_____

PART 5

LEADING AND BELONGING

CHAPTER 32

The Kaizen Executive

[E-Mail from Tom]

Alan, here are some thoughts about the difference between crisis-driven and kaizen-driven executives. It's a little wicked, but not inaccurate, I think. Feel free to circulate, add to, comment, whatever. —Tom.

In a crisis-driven system, the executives tend to be those who were "right" fastest and most often at school and work—especially in the eyes of those who graded and promoted them. Being "different" or "wrong" meant that one was weeded out from among the preferred. In turn, the "right" ones became successful in organizations led by the prior generation of those who, in their time, were also "right." Being raised in such environments, it was only natural for executives to think that anyone who did not think and act as they did must be "wrong."

Most employees in this type of system spend endless hours trying to figure out how to get along with the boss without sounding like spineless yes-men and -women. Long meetings, energy, and the dollars represented by them are squandered in second-guessing what the highly judgmental crisis-driven boss wants to hear. Elaborate presentations hide or obscure the real issues in order to appear to be "right" and on top of things. No one wants to receive the harsh judgment of an opinionated and self-righteous executive, especially when that person has the power to demote, pass over, or even fire. The game is "Try to think like the boss, but appear to have arrived at the same conclusions independently."

Crisis-driven bosses always want that kind of response, since they believe they have the right answer. After all, they became the boss because they were right. But they don't like toadies, because it's "wrong" to be a toadie.

It is very difficult, but not impossible, to think almost exactly like someone else. Learning to do it, however, drives out one's own inner sense of what is appropriate for any given situation. Employees playing this game become incapable of initiating change or leading any significant improvement. They have lost faith in their own ability to see and think for themselves. They question themselves, since for years "seeing things differently" has been deemed wrong.

When you are told for years that different is wrong, you no longer trust what you may once have thought you knew. Without trusting what you know, you cannot take initiative or leadership. Anxiety and frustration take over and blaming the boss or others becomes the major outlet. I am not saying that anything goes, that there are no incorrect or mistaken ideas, but the punitive and negative approach of crisis-driven systems makes "agreeing with the established right way," or "groupthink" the governing process in managerial relations. Improvement through experimenting, risk taking, innovation, and other approaches requiring interpersonal trust are driven out of the system.

In contrast, kaizen-thinking executives have a strong vision of how an improving organization could look. Theirs is not a vision of numbers and profits, but one of human operations. They see clearly, as if they are already realized, the qualities and practices of themselves and others that nurture and sustain innovation, experimentation, honesty, resourcefulness, initiative, mutual respect, and continuous learning. Ideas are treated as resources or raw materials to be developed and applied, rather than being judged immediately as right or wrong. Curiosity about how someone is thinking about technology, customers, or products is as important as the conclusions. How the collective human system is performing takes precedence over outstanding individual accomplishment. Presentations are simple, clear and to the point, and people are encouraged to state what they see and why. New ideas are welcomed from all quarters, because these executives know that in an open system, meritless ideas soon fall of their own weight.

Above all, kaizen-thinking executives know the power of themselves as models. They know that employees watch what they do more than what they say. Kaizen-thinking executives never make the assumption that they will be excused for not following through on commitments because their intentions were good. They endeavor to minimize or eliminate anger, vindictiveness, impatience, sarcasm, humiliation and threats, and hypocrisy or double standards from their dealings with others, because they know that such behavior undercuts and eventually destroys a culture that supports improvement. Making many people feel valued and eager to make even greater strides forward is the aim. Based upon good data, disagreements about direction are openly discussed. Common directions are sought and undermining of others is not permitted.

Because they think systemically, these executives are constantly making connections and building bridges across functions. Seeming differences are orchestrated into harmonious overall performance. Multiple facets of work are demonstrably appreciated by showing their connection and importance to overall goals, while the desire to differentiate is replaced by encouragement to find common ground.

Kaizen-thinking executives are always learning, optimistic about improvement and change. They know things can and will get better with proper support. They believe in a world that is evolving through a complex series of balances and counterbalances. There are no disasters and no "home runs" for these executives, for theirs is a growing sense that all of us working together will figure things out and improve as we go. They impart that confidence to the people who work with them. They inspire others with confidence that survival is a given and that growth and excellence are the challenge.

As in everything else, Crisis-driven executive leadership appears to be the easy way. It is self-centered, withdrawn, judging the rightness or wrongness of the ever-intruding world, as though the executive were not an integral part of that world, playing an active part in creating that which is being judged. In contrast, kaizen executives get involved in the work of leading people by becoming involved with them. They see the reality that others see and the issues that concern them without losing their own balance and systemic awareness. Their role is one of weaving the best with the best and encouraging their acting together. They pay attention to themselves with grace and humility, and to others with care and compassion.

Comments and Reflections

CHAPTER 33

Crisis-Driven vs Kaizen Leadership

Tom: Growing up, I can recall having one kaizen leader. He was my high school algebra teacher. I disliked the guy because he made me work harder than I wanted to, but I respected him because he cared enough to prevent me from doing poorly in algebra. He was the only teacher who would give tests over and over and coach those who wanted it until they passed the test. His idea of teaching was to have no failed student unless the student wanted to fail. He was willing to work with us, doing whatever was necessary to help us understand how algebra worked. Most of my other teachers judged our work as it fit or didn't fit the concepts they presented. Their objective was to have a nice neat curve from A to F. I became convinced that the shape of the curve was more important than we were.

Crisis-driven leadership is of two types. First, there is the supervisor who judges our actions and behaviors. And second, there is the perfectionist who always points out where we are deficient. The classic supervisor oversees our actions with an eye to keeping us in line, under control, doing the right thing. The supervisor is trying to get standards met as the ultimate goal. Variances from standard in behavior prompt corrective action. So long as everyone is doing what he or she is told, the supervisor can sit back and oversee.

There are few of these traditional supervisors left in the world, thank goodness. It's dehumanizing to be treated in this manner, and we are moving away from its practice. Many people believe that is the problem with U.S. industry—that we have gotten soft and need to "get tough" again. The fact is, this type of supervising is totally non-value added and only creates extra cost.

The perfectionist as leader will always be first to point out shortcomings compared to where we have to be. Setting direction or raising sights is necessary in good leadership, but when the direction is used only to illustrate inadequacies it becomes demoralizing leadership. This type of leader, as with most perfectionists, is usually fearful of his own failure and thinks that constant reminding of the shortcomings of himself and others will push everyone to excel. Perfectionists work only on the concept level and can always have a more correct version of what should or should not be done. By staying on the concept level, they don't have to expose their inability to make anything happen. When pushed hard, they will drop down to the action level and become a supervisor-type leader. They have no sense of operational or system level thinking to lead from. They give grades, but no help for improvement.

Alan: It seems to me that there is a third type who must always be out in front, whether that be in having the best ideas or in making decisions. I once had a boss who just couldn't tolerate not being the smartest, most decisive person in the organization. He constantly complained about the lack of brains and initiative among the rest of his staff, but it was very clear from his actions and words that nobody had better preempt his position at the head of the group.

Tom: Yes, that's a pretty common type, especially in highly competitive environments. I think it's a variety of the second type I have identified, but we could treat it as a third type just because it is so common. In any case, the people under such a leader get demoralized, don't they?

Alan: Certainly, or they just get resigned to waiting until the next set of complaints is aired and the next set of orders given.

Tom: It's a very different situation under kaizen leadership. The kaizen leader has equally high ideas about excellence, but realizes that achievement of continuous improvement is a matter of upgrading systems and improving operations to get results. This type of leader excels at asking questions to get people to think about aspects of the system that do not support excellence. He or she constantly seeks data concerning operational malfunctions, not for the purpose of judging, but in order to clarify what has to be improved. Dysfunctional individual actions are viewed as outcomes of old habits, systemic reinforcements, or basic beliefs, and the cause is always pursued. Nor are kaizen leaders afraid to trace the possible cause back to their own behaviors or demands, since such investigations lead to opportunities for their own growth and improvement. Leaders like my algebra teacher want to have no human failures in their organizations. They seek data when people are not performing, and they make clear the ways to success. Then, if individuals choose not to work on improving, they know why they can no longer be retained. It is ultimately their choice, but that choice is a source of regret to the leader.

Crisis-driven leadership can be hard or soft in terms of holding people accountable. "Hard" and "soft" are both terms used in crisis-driven systems. The hard leader judges harshly and demands results. The soft leader judges mildly and requests results. In both cases results are primary, but with hard leaders, if the results are not achieved, people are discarded. With soft leaders, on the other hand, if results are not achieved, excuses and promises are made, and no one learns anything—except perhaps a certain contempt for the leader.

Kaizen leadership concerns itself with asking good questions, finding what's not aligned or connected, coaching for improvement from wherever the individual begins, listening intently and with a "third ear," and being clear and concise about what's needed. "Hard" and "soft" are meaningless terms since they do not add value or lead to improvement; they describe leaders' personal styles, rather than characteristics of an improvement process.

Finally, crisis-driven leaders love to be the "boss," as you identified in your third type. They need to show off their discriminating mind through judging the ideas of others. They need to show people they know more and better about what needs to be done. They want to stand out, stand in front, lead the charge, ride the white horse, and single-handedly win the game! They seem to believe that the development of others is detrimental to their control and a sign of weakness. As followers, we frequently collude in this stance by idolizing the crisis-driven hero—the frontier marshall who kills the bad guy and saves the pitifully weak townfolk (ourselves). It's so much easier and less risky. There are no heroes in continuously improving systems— or on second thought, it's probably more accurate to say that all of us are heroes in these systems, but heroes of a very different sort.

Comments and Reflections

CHAPTER 34

Leading the Shift To Total Quality

Tom: We are obsessed by our desire never to fail and always to be right. I saw this clearly for the first time when I was about thirteen. My father was a perfectionist about everything around the house. Every summer I had the chore of cutting and trimming the grass. For years I tried to do it "right," that is, to my father's standard. I always failed. One day I decided to go all-out on the cutting job. After hours of meticulous work on a small lawn I was satisfied that the job was picture perfect. When my father arrived home he took one look and criticized everything I had done. In a flash I realized that there was something wrong with this whole game of "I try to do it right and always fail." In frustration I blurted out that if he didn't like it, he should do it himself.

After he tired of chasing me with a broom handle, I realized with horror the treason I had committed. I thought that surely I was doomed to wander the streets of Pittsburgh a homeless waif. But of course he soon forgot the incident and things returned to normal.

Reflecting on the event, however, I saw that my father was a perfectionist regarding anything I did. He was not looking to get the grass cut well or to help me improve. He was looking for opportunities to criticize, judge, and control my behavior. He clearly thought that if I ever did something "right," that is, pleasing to him, I would quit trying to do better. His good intention was making me crazy through my inability to please him. I wasn't sure I was smart, but I knew I could figure out how to cut grass! The key point I am making, though, is that the quality of the work was secondary to his need to build my character through judging and controlling.

Alan: That's a lot like what we managers do in trying to achieve quality in our organizations. We become so attached to our analytical judgments and our need to control that we forget we are here together to create an organization that will survive, just as your father forgot what a home and parental guidance were for.

Tom: Organizational quality is achieved through constant improvement in creating all aspects of the system. Constant improvement is necessary, because achieving quality of process is like aiming at a constantly moving target. Crisis-driven thinking, on the other hand, seems easier, because it is based on some fixed standard, like 100%. We usually think the standard is perfection, but when asked for a description we cannot really describe it. This is the source of the familiar line, "I don't know what's right but I'll know it when I see it."

Perfectionists don't really care about an improvement process. They demand the indescribable perfect state now—which is an immature wish for some magic way to get results without work or through superhuman efforts by others. A perfectionist is like an unhappy child who wants the world to drop everything and make him or her feel better immediately. Although such people complain the loudest and strongest about quality, they are unwilling to work toward developing it. Instead, they try to threaten subordinates into better performance.

Alan: I didn't know you knew the man I used to work for!

Tom: The organizational shift to a drive for developing quality must replace the many personal and systemic messages that constantly judge failure and do nothing to develop capability. To lead that process is to begin to dismantle the negative failure messages and create messages that enhance change and improvement. Line and staff functions all play roles in this process, since so many different messages exist in so many places. The most common crisis-driven message is the one calling for cost reduction. How this usually works is that someone reports *after the fact* that we spent too much money, and then goes after the guilty party or parties. As in all crisis-driven systems, the money is already spent, and we chase down symptoms of cost rather than the deeper causes.

Alan: And we never take note of how much it costs in staff time and effort to do cost studies.

Tom: A kaizen approach to quality looks at the whole system and figures out why so much cost is incurred. The objective is not to find someone to blame, but rather to understand the causes. From that understanding, major and minor changes can be made to improve total quality. In this case, total quality is defined as the best way we can operate to do the best possible work we can right now. Learning through this process opens new doors, and quality sights are raised.

Alan: The other thing that happens when a report says that costs are too high is the old exercise of cost cutting, which almost always involves people in the guilty department or division losing their jobs. Then, instead of being able to investigate why costs are so high, the very people who could be most helpful in rooting out those causes are no longer with the organization. Frequently the result is that there are fewer people to do the work, with all the inefficiencies still intact, and, because of increased work loads, more mistakes and omissions occur—which causes costs to rise still further.

Tom: As leaders of ourselves and others in making this shift to total quality, we must be able to look at situations without knee-jerk reactions and without judgment and blaming. This is especially true of looking at ourselves. If we can look only to judge, we cannot keep up the energy for improvement. In such a case, efforts to improve take second place to the need to be right and judge the wrong. If we can't make the switch, we will gather more and more data, use it to judge and blame, and become more and more paralyzed by thoughts of our stupidity. The data simply tell us how the system currently performs. It is here that we must begin the improvement process. Interpreting the data as telling us we are bad or wrong or stupid tempts us strongly to deny the situation.

Alan: To the Crisis-driven person, just looking at the world unflinchingly as it is and not being upset is not enough. Somehow one has to be anguished before quality can be created.

Tom: Yes. I could never comprehend how my father thought that getting angry at me would result in a better lawn. The kaizen approach to quality sees nothing but positive opportunity in all situations. The need to be innocent or blameless is not important. If the company doesn't produce a quality product at low cost, on time, it won't do that any better if people get angry and blame one another or feel bad about it. That is to deny the wholeness of the system. In our desire to be individuals we have lost the sense of interdependence. You cannot have independent quality in some parts, but not in others, and expect quality to emerge from the whole interdependent system. Leaders need to be able to ask questions of the system and hear the response without blaming.

Comments and Reflections

_____

_____

_____

_____

_____

CHAPTER 35

Commitment at Work

Alan: The question of commitment is raised quite often in today's workplace. I am constantly hearing or reading about workers' lack of commitment to their employers or to the company.

Tom: Yes, I find that most people use the word to describe some assumed way of working, rather than a description of a human process.

Alan: What do you mean?

Tom: For me, commitment means the will to expend energy toward some end or achievement, to be excited or energized into giving myself in a dedicated manner. Instead, I find that people talk of individuals being committed, or not, without clarifying what they are committed to.

Alan: So you question the validity of what we might call commitment as a generalized state of being. The question always has to be asked, committed to what? It also sounds as though you would classify something like "the company" as too abstract to carry much meaning.

Tom: I think so, particularly when we are dealing with extremely large corporations that employ thousands of people and are managed impersonally, perhaps by people who live halfway around the world. I find that everyone I talk to has strong commitments; the question is, to what? I myself at times have used the term "highly committed workforce" without being clear as to exactly what the commitment was about. Did it mean commitment to quality, to making money, to getting ahead, to survival, or what? It may have meant all of those things to different people at different times. No wonder it's so difficult to create a "committed workforce!"

Defining our commitments and owning them is critical to our working and relating well with each other. In my life I have often been accused of not wanting to make a commitment. What was really meant in that context was that I didn't, and don't, want to commit to the concept of marriage. I have chosen instead to be committed to helping others achieve more of their potential at work and in their living. This is what has captured my energy. I think that each of us can reflect on what it is that gives us that heightened sense of energy and dedication—something we never tire of doing, discussing, or contemplating.

Alan: What religious people refer to as a "calling" or "vocation"?

Tom: Possibly. In the workplace the difficulty is that executives, managers, and shop-level employees all have different commitments that are not clearly defined and owned, much less integrated. They all may have some generalized commitment to the survival of the organization, but does that really energize people on a day-to-day basis? Making money for the company is another commitment widely affirmed by managers, but I doubt that it serves anyone as a day-to-day energizer. Unfortunately, too many people have unconsciously committed themselves to doing well financially, or gaining status or power. If raised to consciousness, those commitments are defended as the only legitimate ones, based on the idea that individuals pursuing their own self-interest will create a capable organization. With such an orientation, the job of executives is to align self-interest rewards with the good of the customer and the total organization. This tactic may be made to work, but it creates significant inefficiencies.

Alan: I have known of several companies, and a lot of sales divisions, organized around these principles. They are fiercely competitive, internally as well as externally. The managers have to be a bit like wild-animal trainers, constantly cracking the whip and making sure that no one gets behind them.

Tom: The bottom line is whether we can commit to the idea and action of supporting, helping and giving to others, and receiving help in return. It is a commitment to give first, rather than to get first. Commitments to get first serve only to pull us apart, separate our energies, and pit us against each other in competitive striving. The commitment to give unites, pulls us together, and breaks down barriers. Yet we cannot do it all alone; we need also to receive from others, graciously and gratefully.

When we give to customers, our peers and our workers, the system works better. The "get" commitment sets up an atmosphere of scarcity. This scarcity idea creates greater and greater competition among ourselves and leads to distrust and overall system breakdown. We can choose to commit to giving, or to getting. In a system that seems to choose only getting, giving sometimes feels like putting yourself at a disadvantage, but the commitment to giving is its own reward. It will also uncover a world not based on scarcity, but rather on abundance. From that you will receive more than you ever expected.

Comments and Reflections: What bearing does this chapter have on the increasing practice of hiring "temps" or "peripherals" instead of permanent employees? What's the difference between hiring people who want to work only part time because it better suits their needs and patterns of living, and hiring for part-time work those who want and need fulltime employment?

CHAPTER 36

Stewardship and Ownership

Tom: Many of the "simpler" cultures, like those of the Native American tribes, seem to have had no concept of ownership of the land or nature. They saw themselves as participants in the natural order of things—creatures along with all the others, mutually interdependent. This consciousness allowed them to live harmoniously with their surroundings. The concept of ownership that rules so much of our living could use some balance with that of stewardship. This is true in the work environment, as well as in our personal experience.

Alan: I know a lot of attention has been paid recently to the notion of stewardship over the natural environment in response to acid rain, the ozone layer depletion, urban pollution, and global warming. But what do you mean about stewardship in the workplace and with respect to ourselves?

Tom: First of all, stewardship simply means having the responsibility to care for or maintain something that is not yours to do with as you please. In many large organizations, much struggle, pain, and lack of improvement occur because so much energy is used to defend what we think of as "rightfully ours." At the primary levels people have "their" jobs, "their" machines, "their" tools, etc. Higher up we have managers talking about "their" departments, "their" people, "their" budgets. Even at the top, it becomes "their" company, "their" division, "their" product.

Alan: What's wrong with that? I've always been told that strong ownership feelings create commitment to and caring for things.

Tom: I find that a strong sense of ownership that means possession rather than stewardship leads to abuse and misuse. Owners who believe that "my possessions are mine to do with as I please" disconnect themselves from their surroundings. They try to erect a (false) boundary to protect and isolate what is theirs from what is not theirs. The idea seems to be to see how much stuff—money, people, things—they can possess. The higher the pile of accumulated stuff, the more worthy the possessor is supposed to be.

Alan: There's a popular bumper sticker that reads, "He who dies with the most toys wins." And corporate CEOs are rewarded handsomely for greater and greater profitability. It seems that in our culture we believe strongly in what you call ownership-as-possession.

Tom: It does seem so. But when we have translated financial status and material possessions into inherent worthiness, we have lost sight of our own humanity. Then people are equated with costs and money. That lets us do anything, if the price is right. In factories the possession/worthiness game plays out in unwillingness to share resources, tools, and energy because sharing feels like giving possessions away for nothing and enhancing someone else. Everything gets translated into an economic model. At its worst, people in positions of power over others come to believe they have ownership rights. When we believe we own something and can do with it as we wish by right of ownership, the door to abuse is opened. You don't have to seek far for people who don't have much patience with problematic possessions, whether things or people. Their solution is to discard, replace, or beat into submission. This idea of ownership plays right into the managerial need to control. We believe we have more control when we own things or people. Let's see, we are against slavery, aren't we?

Alan: We had a job-posting system in a place where I worked, but it didn't operate in one department because the manager thought all the employees there belonged to her. She made it clear to all "her" people that if they applied for a job outside "her" department and didn't get it, they might as well quit the company, because she wouldn't tolerate "disloyal" employees.

Tom: In our personal being, this need to own plays out around owning ideas that we must defend, owning roles that we must protect, owning identities that we must preserve, owning children that must reflect glory on us through their achievements. Owning their physical, intellectual, and emotional parts is how we think we control them. What we don't see is that the very owning process, linked with a need to control outcomes, is the chief cause of our being out of touch with our children and ourselves. When we are out of touch, we are out of control of our being in process—that is,"living" or "being alive."

Alan: In other words, we can own these various fixed concepts of ourselves and others, or we can live and let others live. But we can't have it both ways.

Tom: That's it. In contrast to owning, stewardship is understanding that we are entrusted with ourselves and others, with tools, machines, buildings, energy, and so on, that need to be maintained and developed to serve a higher purpose. Accumulation and possession of these things is not a higher purpose! In a plant or office, the issue is not how big your organization is, but whether we are doing all we can with the resources entrusted to us to serve our customers. It is knowing that as managers we cannot constantly, personally, control serving the customers, but must depend on our organization—its people, systems, structures, and processes—to deliver the required products or services on time at the right price. Our job as stewards is to nurture, maintain, and grow the capability of all these elements to serve the customer. Seeing ourselves as stewards of material and human assets produces a very different awareness from that of seeing ourselves as their owners and controllers.

On the shop or office floor, we want people to "take care" of the customer. We want people to "take care" of their tools, workspace, machines, material, etc. We expect this. But most of the models of management are models of "my" department, "my" plant, "my" people, "my" company. Virtually everyone wants to show what he or she controls and therefore how important he or she is. Bosses act like they don't have time to take care of the organization or people, yet somehow they want "their" people to "take care" of the customer. Often the reason they give for not taking care of the organization or its people is that they are too busy taking care of the customer's complaints. But the reason why employees are not taking care to satisfy the customer in the first place is that they are too busy trying to establish control over what they own—their job, their self-respect, their seniority. The traditional adversarial labor/management contract is an extreme example of contracted ownership.

Alan: You mean because the contract spelled out what exclusively belonged to management and what belonged to labor in the form of wages, hours, working conditions, job classifications, and grievance procedures?

Tom: Exactly. Managers tend to forget that an organization is simply a complex tool that they have been entrusted with, to take care of and enable to work well in responding to customer needs.

Alan: As I understand your use of "take care of," you don't mean it paternalistically. The meaning you give it includes both service to something or someone, and caring for that thing or person.

Tom: Yes. Stewardship caring is a high regard and respect for the resource and for the people being served. Stewardship is humbling because it derives from respect for the great power for good of those resources, and the great responsibility bestowed upon their steward to bring forth that good in the best possible way.

In our own being we are stewards of our lives; we don't own them, although most of us treat our lives as merely another possession—and not a very highly valued one at that. I cannot answer who the owner is, but it is certainly a good question to ponder. So too with the corporation. The CEO does not own a public corporation, the shareholders do. But who are the shareholders? Investment and insurance companies and pension funds usually hold controlling shares these days. But whose money buys these shares? All the people who invest and work in the system. So we own the corporation but don't own the corporation—at the same time!

Alan: Isn't it ironic that CEOs will export jobs to low-wage countries in the name of shareholders when many of the shareholders are the very employees being laid off? But as you point out, they are hidden behind another group, such as a mutual fund, whose demand for higher profits drives the CEO to take the actions he or she does. On the personal level, we see women arguing for legalized abortion because they claim they own their bodies and therefore have an absolute right to do what they want with the fetus. And on the other side there are those who refute this argument by claiming that the father, or society at large, owns the unborn infant. In either case, the notion of stewardship is disregarded in favor of that of ownership. Yet stewardship goes way beyond this simple argument. It negates all the traditional notions of ownership: that husbands own their wives, or that fathers own their children—or, in fact, that anyone owns anyone else. Stewardship puts this whole issue on a different footing entirely.

Tom: That's true. On one hand, we are responsible for "owning" our being here and who we are. On the other hand, we are formed and created to a major extent by our biological inheritance and by our social/cultural/family conditioning. Both are true. To become stewards of our own lives in this paradoxical state is to take great care of how we are becoming: not to abuse ourselves through harsh self-judging, but to nurture our gifts as appreciating assets, and to realize we are inherently valuable; not to expose ourselves needlessly to psychological and physical attack, but to provide ourselves with care and protection from harsh environments; not to limit growth, but to do what is required to nourish internal growth; not to waste energy on ownership questions, but to invest energy in pursuit of the purpose we serve.

Comments and Reflections

PART 6

CHAPTER 37

Considering Customers

[One night over dinner]

Alan: Have you noticed that more and more companies are claiming to be "customer oriented," "led," "driven," or otherwise sensitive to customer needs? I'm skeptical that there's much substance behind the hype.

Tom: Me, too. But I'm interested in the reasons for your skepticism.

Alan: It's based not only on negative experiences with companies that make such a claim, but more on my own experience that grasping someone else's reality requires considerable work and effort. Most companies seem to be primarily concerned with maximum profit margins. So they look at customers solely with one question in mind: what they can do for me? Sellers don't really care to help customers with their struggle to improve what they are trying to do or how they are trying to live.

Tom: Your point reminds me of a co-worker. She was generally viewed as a stereotypical helper, you know the kind I mean? She was always willing to subordinate her needs to those of others. She often complained of being put upon, but continued doing for others and never letting others do for her.

She and I became close friends—at least I thought so—often talking together about work, life and relationships. One day she became visibly upset and demanded, "What do you want from me?"

Startled, I replied that I wanted nothing more than her friendship and that she did not have to "do" anything to earn mine. She could not tolerate this setup. Apparently she was confused because she didn't know how to act if she couldn't give me what I wanted.

Then I realized that she was not sacrificial and considerate of others, as I had originally thought. Instead, she was trying to control what she got out of relationships, by discovering others' needs and serving them, to put those others in her debt. She was distraught that she couldn't deal with me on the same basis. She was more interested in preserving her control than finding out who I really was.

In time, because she was willing to put our relationship on a different footing by giving up her need to control me through serving, we became true friends and have remained so ever since.

The story illustrates what you have contended already, that most of us generally consider our own needs, and only superficially consider those of others. We are stuck with the notion that we are the center of the universe, and do not or cannot see ourselves as part of a much larger integrated system. To consider others is to start to get a notion of that broader system. It is also a way to discover how much we are all alike.

In a business setting, truly considering customers means knowing what it is like to be in their business, with their issues and their thinking about what they are trying to do. In most cases, however, we are mainly concerned with their impressions of our product or service, not with their ultimate success. Naturally we want and need our company to be successful. But most of us don't fully understand that if our customers do not succeed, we cannot succeed. We think it's enough to meet them at the boundary between our business and theirs and exchange our product or service for their money. Nothing can be farther from a truly healthy business relationship and larger economy. Both are profoundly interdependent.

Alan: In the transportation company where I worked, we had a very large and important customer that also had a sizable fleet of trucks, so in a way they were in competition with us. They had a complicated distribution network, because their plants produced different products all over the United States, and these products had to find their way to warehouses in all the lower 48 and Canada. In serving their needs as suppliers, we had a problem similar to their own: how to distribute their products in the most efficient way.

Some of our systems people literally went to work for that company for a year and came up with a computerized distribution model, which, when implemented, saved our customer over a million dollars a year. We charged them nothing for the service, because we knew that if the model worked for them it would also work for us, and the additional good will generated would stand us in good stead as suppliers. I think this illustrates partnership in action, as well as the effort involved in being truly customer oriented.

Tom: That's an impressive story. And I'm thinking that on the personal level the same principles apply. Many of us want things like recognition, appreciation, love, money, work, and sex from others without giving to or considering them. Most of us will also deny that we act this way because we are taught that such actions are selfish, and selfish is bad. At the same time we are taught that we are independent, unrelated selves, missing the fact that we are inescapably bound up with one another. Much "pop" psychology encourages this unrelated, center-of-the-universe approach by stressing "Take care of No. 1," "Be clear on your demands/needs," "Learn to get what you want." This approach denies the systemic nature of the human condition, yet many follow it. Under the influence of the advice of such "experts," we find ourselves in a standoff with our fellows. We say or think, "You give to me first and then I'll see whether what I have gotten is worth some kind of response from me."

Proponents of this scarcity-oriented, one-up way of dealing with others suggest that if all of us work at getting what we want, everything will be as it should be. The dilemma is that if we are all trying to get, there is no one left to give.

Many of us have lost faith in a future return from a current gift, as was the case in your story. At its most powerful, this faith also holds that it's okay not to get anything in return, that the gift is in the very act of giving. Giving makes the human system work better. This does not mean that there is no room for self-assertion, nor does it mean that to give is good and to receive is bad, as the woman in my story seemed to believe. It simply recognizes that our quality of life is not purely an individual affair. Upgrading the whole human system around us upgrades the quality of everyone's living.

Alan: Connecting back to customers, we need to give their well-being as much consideration as we do our own, because in fact they're the same. We don't and can't exist without them. We are part of a mutually reliant system. Parts may leave and be replaced, but not without pain and loss, so continual improvement of that system is a key management role. When we learn truly to consider customers' needs, we are able to see those needs of our own that once we served under the guise of being customer driven. Inability to see the self-serving dimensions of our own actions makes it impossible to upgrade the whole.

Exercise in thinking about customers' needs. Think about your two or three major customers. These may be internal customers: fellow employees who receive your work and depend on it in order to do their own; or they may be external customers who use and pay for your products or services.

On a sheet of paper jot down everything you know about these customers. For example, how do they use your product or service?

Do they have to rework or adjust it in any way to make it more usable? (Do you know, or are you guessing?) What are they struggling with in their own work? Could you do something about your work that would make things easier for them? Who are their customers? If your customer is a different company, what do you know about it? If you find you don't know the answer to questions like these, ask your customer and build your knowledge/information base.

Ask yourself why. It may possibly be because you are afraid you will build up expectations in your customers that you don't know how to meet, or perhaps because the answer will make you feel guilty or incompetent. Be aware of the feelings but don't give in to them. Ask yourself instead, what can I do about changing the situation?

CHAPTER 38

Impressing
the Public

[Driving to the airport after a seminar]

Alan: Seeing all these billboards with their messages of "drink this" and "smoke that and you'll really be special" just drive me nuts!

Tom: (chuckling) Yeah? Why is that?

Alan: Advertising has made such an art of deception. It's not just the products either. People and businesses want us to believe that the concepts they profess are actual descriptions of who they are or what they are selling. In essence they try to manage the impressions we have of them. Now, I know this deception is not usually malicious, although sometimes it is taken to harmful extremes. But the idea that one can fool people into buying something other than what's really being sold leads inevitably to making the quick sale, then "getting out of town," and, in the personal world, to broken relationships. I'm thinking of a billboard advertising an insurance company in my home town that proclaims, "We Care About You." Every time I see that sign I think, "Yeah, sure you do." Well, maybe it's true, you know? But I have gotten so jaded by that kind of stuff, I automatically react negatively.

Tom: The effects of deception, as you say, are destroyed relationships. Yet it is practiced everywhere, not just in advertising. This fact was illustrated vividly for me one time after I had gone through an extremely intense personal experience. I had spent a week in a group where, for the first time in my life, I let others in on what I considered my deepest secret: that I spent an enormous amount of energy trying to convince people that I was intelligent, liberal, sensitive—presenting these various fronts to conceal what I thought was an unacceptable inner self. After confronting and discarding the false self I was projecting, I found that I had much more energy available to become some of those things I professed and truly wanted to be.

On returning home, I went to a Halloween party with friends. As I watched them take off their party masks, I saw for the first time that my friends were still wearing masks, just as I had. I was amazed that I hadn't seen this before. Later I realized that I had used all my attention and energy to keep my own mask in place and was never able truly to look at anyone else. Trying to manage the impression others had of me did not allow me clearly to see either myself or them as we actually were.

As customers, we know that many products and services fall far short of their advertised claims. Most good salespersons know that the best sales tool is an excellent product; there is no need to push or make the hard sell. Knowing this, the Japanese auto industry aimed at producing high-quality cars early on. Their first attempts failed rather badly, but they learned from their mistakes, made significant improvements, and soon had no trouble breaking into the U.S. market, rapidly gaining widespread acceptance.

Alan: In contrast, American auto manufacturers continued to rely on advertising hype that only infuriated and made cynics out of customers whose expectations were repeatedly dashed by unhappy experiences. Can we say the same of interpersonal relationships?

Tom: Certainly. But between individuals, managing impressions takes more subtle forms. We conceptualize ourselves and others, trying to play out scenarios depicting how our relationships *should* work. Rather than a real person-to-person conversation, we usually have a conversation between my concept of me and my concept of you. Meanwhile, the other is doing the same thing, and neither of us notices that we are making no real connection. In this process of talking to and from our self-concepts, we never see each other's true being hidden behind our masks.

At work, bosses try to act like their concept of "boss" toward their concept of "employee." Leaders try to act out concepts of leading. The result is deception, both of others and of the deceiver. When you realize that a synonym of "deceive" is "mislead" you can see the serious mischief at work here. Not only do billboard ads mislead, leaders do too. And as we said before, deception and manipulation breed distrust and destroy relationships. If the deceivers themselves are deceived by their image management, their inner coherence is destroyed and they literally wind up alienated from themselves.

When we turn ourselves and others into concepts, we treat ourselves and others as objects. Objects, like concepts, are not alive. Therefore, when we make persons into objects, we are creating an artifact, a dead thing. Not to see our own life or that of another directly is to lose the ability to grow and develop, since only something that's alive can grow. As concepts or objects we have no living reality from which to start, so we're stuck.

Alan: Once I spent a couple of days in a fraternity house. Every one of the members had been slotted into a character role. There was the "animal-jock," who punched holes in the wall when he was drunk; the "intellectual;" the "poor, hardworking architect," and so on. They were all held in these roles by the expectations of their brothers.

Tom: Subjects, who are alive, are capable of growing and changing. Businesses that do not see their own operation clearly and openly, like these persons we've been discussing, cannot develop capability, since they too have objectified themselves. Moreover, a business that regards customers as merely purchasers and makes them objects, cannot see them clearly in the context of their own struggles, and cannot satisfy their needs in the long run. Such businesses are living on borrowed time, because eventually a competitor will appear on the scene who will enter into the customers' reality and satisfy their needs.

Alan: I know what you're saying, and I also know that it's very hard not to hold onto concepts of myself that I have held for a long time. For example, my father used to call me a "clumsy ox." Whenever I drop something or try to handle things with gloves on, that term springs to mind. And as a result of reading a lot of self-help literature, I have tried to form a positive self-image to take the place of the early negative ones. But I must confess that the old "clumsy ox" tape is still there, so I try to cover it up with other disguises.

Tom: To most of us the notion of not trying to live up to a positive self-concept—or not trying to live down a negative one—is to give up. Actually, "trying" is the culprit here: it is a form of self-manipulation by which we make a "project" of ourselves. In doing so we deny the fact that we are constantly becoming and are always other than what we imagine ourselves to be. If we are not diverted by "trying," we can be directly in touch with our growth process and can see how to help it along. Others with clear sight have seen through our masks all along. We aren't fooling anyone but ourselves.

Alan: A therapist friend of mine once demonstrated the futility of trying by giving me a ball and telling me to try throwing it. At first I just threw it. He said, "No, no. I told you to try throwing it. You threw it. Now *try* throwing it. I got the point. Just as you say, trying gets in the way of seeing and doing. But I believe it is difficult for us trying-oriented, conceptual people to grasp your point and practice awareness of it.

Comments and Reflections

CHAPTER 39

Quality is a
Feminine Art

Tom: Quality is a feminine art.

Alan: Now there's a statement that should raise some questions and eyebrows! Why do you say that?

Tom: Because I'm getting clearer about the connections between quality, wholemindedness, and art. Quality involves several elements critical to sustained performance. We have looked at kaizen vs crisis-driven thinking; creation at the moment vs inspection; continuous improvement vs innovation; using the senses vs judgments; capability vs strategic planning; and integration vs fragmentation. All of these elements constitute a mindset capable of achieving high quality in anything we undertake. But the application of these to our own mind is a feminine art. If we try to apply these ideas as a science, traditionally understood as analytical, I'll guarantee you that we will make little or no progress toward a shift in consciousness.

Alan: For us men who like to think we are scientific, that's a pretty daunting statement. What do you mean by a "feminine art"?

Tom: First of all, to me feminine does not mean female. It is no more an exclusive province of women than masculine is an exclusive province of men. Feminine and masculine are metaphors for two aspects of all humans, corresponding roughly to the two hemispheres of the brain. The right, or "feminine," hemisphere deals with holistic images and pictures. It thinks in terms of context and background. It is the side that holds or contains and integrates. The left, or "masculine," hemisphere creates words, symbols, and focal points. It is the logical, sequential side that analyzes, that breaks things down into cause and effect in a neat linear fashion. Wholemindedness is one's ability to access both hemispheres easily. The reason I refer to that ability as feminine is that the right side contains or embraces the left side, but not vice versa. The context contains the focal point, but the point does not contain the context.

Alan: I see—aha! a feminine statement! Are you saying that if we think with our whole brains, whether we are male or female, we are capable of both appreciating contexts and relationships and thinking analytically within those frameworks—rather like being able to read a map and then drive from one point to another on it?

Tom: Yes, we need to view from the feminine perspective so our masculine actions can be appropriate. Actions are "masculine" since they are fragmented and focused. Our feminine guides the masculine action, just as you say in your map/ driving example. This is the underlying premise of the oriental martial arts, and the essence of Taoist philosophy: The feminine can't act; the masculine can't see. We need both working in harmony, since they go with and are necessary to each other. Coming only from our masculine side, we react over and over again without seeing the futility of our efforts. (I have referred throughout to that reaction as the endless fire-fighting that changes nothing.) Some tend to be proud of their "action" orientation without regard to the overall effect.

Alan: In their book *In Search of Excellence,* Thomas Peters and Robert Waterman write approvingly of the approach they called "Ready, Fire, Aim!" (Note that aiming requires sight.) According to you, they were coming from the masculine orientation that argues for doing something even if it's wrong. I once had a (male) student who asserted strongly that it was better to make a wrong decision than no decision at all, on the grounds that doing something is better than doing nothing.

Tom: That is the normal masculine unseeing response that places everything in a do/don't-do framework. I am saying that seeing before doing and linking them together are critical to quality. This is wholemindedness.

I say quality is an art because most of us understand science as based on analysis, predictability, and laws, whereas quality is a process based on probability and learning, or exploring and improving. A law says you must either comply or break it, and predictability is the ability to measure and recreate any phenomenon. Some purely masculine-minded persons have actually said that if you can't measure it and reproduce it, it isn't real. I ask them only to apply that rule to themselves.

Alan: So when you say that quality is an art, you are framing it in contrast to the Newtonian notions most of us older folks were raised with. In the sense you are employing it, art is more closely related to quantum physics in that both deal with probability and freedom of choice.

Tom: Yes, the world understood as mechanism is governed by the Newtonian physics of predictability and laws. That understanding is still useful when we are dealing with large inanimate objects in motion. But as you point out, recent scientific theory contains that and goes beyond to the world of probabilities, tendencies and trends, where freedom and choice seem to play some important part.

As the people in the field put it, high quality is continuously moving, requiring endless learning and experimentation to determine its present direction or location. See the connection?

Alan: Yes, I see. Then can we say that science and art are growing closer together?

Tom: Very possibly. Art's realm is that of the imagination, and therefore of freedom. It is something to experiment with, learn from, adjust, appreciate, integrate, and enjoy. One can say much the same of pure mathematics, but with the latter it must follow its own internal rules. Because it is free, art is not predictable in the simple cause-and-effect way of mechanisms. Yet it too invents and then follows certain conventions—and the uncanny thing about both mathematics and great art is that they have a way of forecasting—perhaps foreseeing is a better term—realities long before they become "science" to most of us. Art is wholeminded. It foreshadows and contains science, but applied science is a product of the left brain, and therefore does not and cannot contain art. Yet one can argue that science, at those points when the great new syntheses break into consciousness, is, and always has been, wholeminded. It may very well be, then, that great art and great science are both rooted in the same mysterious source where the human mind comes into direct and immediate contact with reality.

However, trying to apply masculine cause-and-effect logic to changing or improving ourselves stems from a misuse of obsolete mechanistic physics and cannot create a quality way of being—though it may create a fairly high state of mechanical functioning that gets us by so long as we live in a mechanistic environment. Adopting the feminine approach is to begin to see ourselves with no need to act or do anything about it. This approach shows us how we work. When we see how we work, we can go about doing kaizen, thus increasing our capability to create an integrated being in a state of continuous improvement.

Alan: In other words, we become our own work of art, but one that is never finished?

Tom: What we accomplish as an end result of this process is the place where we are when we come to a halt in the midst of our play—wherever and whenever that is.

Comments and Reflections

A Note on the
Kaizen Institute of America

Founded by Masaaki Imai, lecturer, consultant, and author of *Kaizen: the Key to Japan's Competitive Success* (McGraw-Hill, 1986), the Kaizen Institute (KI) was conceived as an organization dedicated to repatriating the United States' ideas and approaches to industrial production that had become systematized in Japan, but had been all but forgotten in the land of their birth. These systems owed much of their initial conception to Americans, but as Mr. Imai points out, Japanese consultants and industrial leaders had greatly refined, improved upon, and further explored the implications of the Americans' ideas.

In the late 1980s, Mr. Imai lectured on kaizen throughout the United States and consulted here and there with a variety of manufacturing and service organizations. At the same time he began to assemble a group of American consultants who were familiar with the Japanese concepts and systems, and who formed the nucleus of the Kaizen Institute of America.

To be help to U.S. organizations, these consultants realized they had to help make significant changes on the shop floor. Simultaneously, they had to work with top management to bring about changes in their thinking and behavior. That has been KI's approach for the past five years.

KI now consists of a nationwide network of more than twenty-five consultants, linked to each other through a common vision and the principles of the new thinking discussed in this book

For information about the services
of the Kaizen Institute of America contact:
   Ms. Kim Kaddatz
   Kaizen Institute of America
   108 El Reno Cove
   Austin, Texas 78734
   512-261-4900 *(phone)*   512-261-5107 *(fax)*

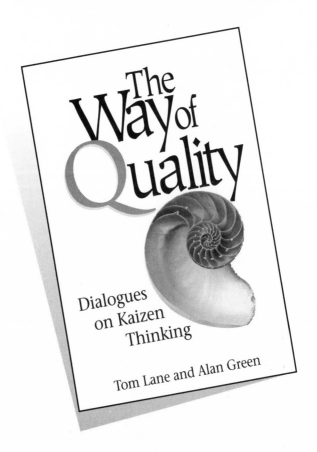